The Transformation Project

A West Michigan Word Weavers Anthology

Contributions by West Michigan Members of

Word Weavers International

Concerning Life Publishing, LLC
Spring Lake, Michigan
www.Concerninglife.org

All biblical references are to the King James Version
unless otherwise expressly noted.

Cover Art by Amber Lauren Striker
Cover Designed by Concerning Life Publishing
Edited by Rachelle Rea (www.RachelleRea.com)

West Michigan Members of Word Weavers International
The Transformation Project

ISBN-10:0988922576
ISBN-13:978-0-9889225-7-0

To my sweet, dear sister-friend — Sharry,

May my story provide inspiration & hope.

Love you,
Teresa ☺

(Jer. 29:11-14)

CONTENTS

FOREWORD

What does it mean to be transformed? Surely not only what we have seen in cartoon characters and comic strips. Or, I should say, surely *more* than that.

Our entire lives are about transformation. Just yesterday as I watched my youngest grandchild go from crawling to walking, I thought of this amazing transformation we have all experienced. We go from dependent infants to giggly, happy-go-lucky children to sullen teenagers to head-strong young adults and finally, should we be so lucky, to wise, mature adults.

And, just as we go from crawling to walking ... from happy-go-lucky to mature in our physical lives, so our life experiences shape us. Change us. *Transform* us.

As Christians we have read and heard countless biblical stories of transformed lives. Moses is transformed from a shepherd of flocks to a shepherd of Hebrew sojourners. Ruth is transformed from despised Moabitess to the great-grandmother of King David. David is transformed from "forgotten son" to the one from whom

God's covenant Son would come.

Peter was transformed from fisher of fish to fisher of men. Saul from murdering tyrant to Paul the Apostle—and one of the most revered figures in history. Mary Magdeline was transformed from demon-tormented to Christ-bringing. And Jews and Gentles were transformed from "little in common" to "One in Him."

The stories go on. Every day. Everywhere. Two thousand years and transformations continue. We, each of us, are transformed by God (sometimes whether we realize it or not), transformed by love, and transformed by life. What you will read within these pages are but a few of those stories.

As one who has watched the transformation of writers over the past seventeen years or more, I pray that as you read this collection of stories from Word Weavers West Michigan members, you will think of your own transformations—both past and future. Because, as I said, we *are* being transformed ... every day. Everywhere.

Eva Marie Everson
President
Word Weavers International, Inc.

Introduction

Transformation. It can occur slowly, as in an evolution or a migration of change. Yet, you experience it in split fragments, in the smallest measurable flashes of time.

In the big picture, you see the mass of micro-changes as a whole. You convince yourself that the transformation occurred in one mighty avalanche, now that the end result is within view.

You stand back. You scan the mountain range. You marvel at its beauty, its grandeur, its foreboding strength, giving little thought to how it came to be. But when you're *in* it, actually a *part* of the transformation, you see all the intricate details of these micro-changes – each separate and unique and profound – like the first snowflakes of winter.

Maybe that's the difference. When you witness transformation in the life of another, you see the result. But when *you* are engaged in the change, it's a bit-by-bit journey that leads to a destination you could not have predicted or prepared for at the onset.

Transformation is continual. It's ongoing. It's an essential part of life. Not just in my life. In your life, too. Don't believe me?

Look at your skin, the largest organ of your body. Go ahead. Pick up a finger – any finger – and stare at it. Hasn't changed all day, has it? It looks the same now as it did 10 years ago…20 years ago….

Oh, really?

Think about the suppleness of your skin – its ability to move and stretch and grow and shrink and heal. It can cool itself with sweat and warm itself with goose bumps, and you're scarcely aware. Think about the fact that it sheds between 30,000 and 40,000 dead cells. Not every year. Not every day. *But every minute of your life.* That's transformation.

Italian actress Sophia Loren was asked once what happens to her within the character that she's asked to portray for any given scene. She put it pretty simply. "The word 'Action!' frees me. The transformation is something I cannot explain – too much analysis might destroy it."

That being said, I have noticed three things about this word that are pretty consistent from person to person:

Transformation comes when you least expect it. I look back at those times in my life, times when the transformation was so obvious that someone might point to me and say, "Wow, you've really changed," and I realize that I had no way to prepare for what was the come.

The illness. The betrayal. The attack. The loss.

You don't expect it. Even if you have signs, you don't think it will ever really happen to you. When you're taken by surprise like this, you can only react to it. And we all know the ugliness of *that* moment. You reel. You fight to gain the life balance that you took for granted just moments before. You must deal with the change now. You can't ignore it.

This is a new experience for you, this transformation that snuck up on you. But now that it's here – now that you're walking around it and examining it from all angles – it's as if your whole world revolves around it. You struggle to remember what life was like before it plopped itself in the middle of your living room, but you just can't remember it ever being any other way.

Transformation comes when you least want it. "Change is good." You've heard that phrase more times that you can count. Then why do you hate it so much? Why do you cringe at the thought? Why do you hold your breath and look the other way, hoping it passes you by?

Because change is hard. *Really hard.* It's uncomfortable. It means learning, often along the most painful paths of life.

So, no. You don't want it. You don't have time for it. You're not up to the challenge. It never asked your permission. Never solicited your opinion. But it's here, just the same.

Transformation comes when you most need it. You cannot grow if you don't change. In fact, the day you stop growing is the day you die.

God's plans for you are mighty. He has people in mind for you to reach, to teach, to bear witness to – people who may not come to know Him through any other means. If He can use your pain, your change, your *transformation* to draw another person in, isn't it worth it?

If this thing called transformation is inevitable – and by the sounds of things it is – why not embrace it? Why not squeeze every drop of life experience out of it?

That's what we tried to do here, in our first ever Word Weavers anthology. We're just a bunch of people from West Michigan who love words, who have something to say, and who have taken the time to examine some of the greater and lesser moments of transformation in our own lives.

Re-live our lessons with us. Celebrate the knowledge, the understanding, and the appreciation we have gained through the process. Breathe in our recounting – whether in short story or in memoir form – just as we offer it.

May these words inspire you to look for those moments of transformation in your own life.

Anna Moore Bradfield
President
West Michigan Word Weavers

Another Metamorphosis

By Cindy Cleaver

It must have been a dream, probably caused by the pressure of graduate study and teaching.

Yesterday, I took a break from my teaching assistant duties in the history department at Notre Dame to call my mother and wish her a Happy 60th Birthday. Before I could get the words out of my mouth, she blurted out, "I quit my job today."

"What?"

"I quit my job today."

"I heard you. I just can't believe it. What are you going to do? You have a good job as a legal secretary. You were going to *retire* from Smith, Adams, and Klein, you said. How could you just *quit* your job?"

"Your Dad and I are moving to Arkansas."

"Huh? When were you going to tell me this?"

"Well, I'm telling you now."

I sat down on my couch, picked up a notebook, and started drawing a woman. Drawing always helps me calm down under duress...and this was duress with a capital D.

I said, "But I am going to school in Indiana."

"I'm fully aware of that, honey. You'll still be able to visit us

1

in Arkansas. It's not as close as Michigan, but it's not as far away as Florida, either. Your grandparents moved to Florida. That was 1,200 miles away."

"How could you decide to move without telling me?"

My mother and I have always been close. She always tells me what she is thinking, even when I don't want to know. Stunned, I started tapping my mechanical pencil, outlining a face, and then adding the nose, the mouth, and the eyes.

"Is it too late to change your mind?"

"Well, we already sold the house, and we closed on the house in Arkansas last week."

"What?" I sputtered. "Last week! You didn't breathe a word of this to me. How could you decide to move without telling me?"

"Your Dad retired in October, and we decided that we could move anywhere we wanted. You remember that Dad went to college and worked in rural churches in Ozark, Arkansas, don't you? He fell in love with the mountains, the hot springs, and just plain folk. So we chose Arkansas. He's been writing those Ozark stories for the last few years. He almost has enough material for a book. You know what they say: 'You can take the boy out of the Ozarks, but you can't take the Ozarks out of the boy.'"

"They do not say that. That is not a saying." I stopped thrumming my pencil, and added my mother's earrings, then the necklace she always wears. "Well, what about Lizzy? Is she going to Arkansas, too?

"No. She's staying in Michigan. She has a great job, and she's been saving money for her own place, and she bought one of those cute one-bedroom condos downtown. One that allows cats. She's taking Tiger with her. That's one problem solved. Cats really don't like moving, you know, especially not three states away."

"But Lizzy has cerebral palsy."

"When has that ever stopped her?"

"She was always going to live with you. How can you

abandon her?"

"Lizzy doesn't want to go to Arkansas. She's an adult. She makes her own decisions."

"You know she can't drive. How is she going to get to work? How is she going to get groceries? I am going to school in Indiana."

"She has that all figured out. She's very capable, you know. That's why she is moving downtown. Work is only a few blocks away, she can shop at the Downtown Market, and most of all, the entertainment is free. She loves Festival and Art Prize. Your aunt, uncle, and cousins live in Grand Rapids, and your brother Eric lives in Lansing. She's worked so hard to be where she is now, and we have no right to stop her from living her life the way she wants to."

I drew her sweater, over a black turtleneck and black pants, shading them in furiously. My mother always wears black pants, because she says they're slimming. That's her opinion.

"How can you leave your Word Weavers group? The feedback, encouragement, and fellowship of fellow writers are priceless. You told me the critiques are a gift. You've been meeting with them twice a month for the last eight years. How can you give that up?"

"I'll miss all of them. But there may be a Word Weavers chapter in Arkansas. And if there isn't, I'll start one."

Drat. I added her glasses. "What about your grandchildren?"

"What grandchildren? None of you is even close to marriage!"

"Eric has a girlfriend. They want to get married and have kids."

"When he has kids, he can bring his family down to Arkansas. They can visit Grandma and Grandpa on the farm, just like I visited my grandparents on the farm."

"A farm! You bought a farm?!"

"Just kidding." I heard Dad laughing in the background. He had been listening on the speaker phone the whole time.

"Just when did you start thinking about moving?"

"On my birthday. Last year."

"Your birth…"

"Honey, I've gotta go. The moving company is calling, and I've been waiting for them to call back. I'll talk to you later."

I added her flats to the picture and paused. Her birthday. When my mother turned 40, she said to my Dad, "No more presents. I want tickets to concerts, plays or comedy acts, and I want you to go with me."

The year she turned 54, we all went to see *The Fiddler on the Roof* at the Civic Theater. But the evening before, on her actual birthday, she went to that Contra dance with my father. The fourth Friday Contra Dance at the urging of their friend, Trinka. She always was a bad influence on my mother, but that is another story. My parents came home exhilarated and repeating to each other, "Then grab your partner, *dosey doe*, swing him/her around and don't let go!" And laughing. My parents are so clumsy. Their dancing is awful, always has been, but Contra dancing is fun, they said. However, twirling triggers my mother's on again, off again episodes of vertigo, so they never went again. They did, however, start going to folk music concerts and community sing alongs.

After the Contra dance, my mother announced, "From now on, I'm gonna try something new on my birthday every year."

That was also the year Mom bought her first new car, a red Chrysler 200. She said, "As long as I can choose the color, I choose red." I couldn't believe it. My mother always chooses blue cars. Blue is her favorite color. But my father confirmed that Mom had always wanted a red car, but when they bought used cars, the color hadn't mattered. The red Chrysler 200 was her answer to her mid-life crisis, she said.

A year of satellite radio came free with the car. My mother

found a bluegrass station and listened to it even when I was in the car, to my disgust. Ugh.

"Why can't you listen to Casting Crowns or Third Day?"

"I like this music. When I was growing up, I sang songs like this with my family. When we went to my grandparents' house, we sang folk songs, and my uncles played along on their electric guitars. It's my car, and I can listen to bluegrass if I want to."

Screeching hyenas and twang.

"I wonder what makes people pick up a banjo or a guitar and practice enough to become good at it." My mother is always wondering this aloud. During our weekly phone calls, she started telling me about her favorite bluegrass groups.

Putting my drawing down on the couch, I walked out to the kitchen to get a cup of tea. Thinking.

When she turned 55, my father had bought them both fly fishing poles and fly fishing lessons. They couldn't do much fishing in March, but she had said, "Anticipation is part of the gift."

I went away to grad school the next year. On her birthday she called to inform me that she had started taking ukulele lessons from my best friend's sister. She had even played a song for me. The next project was to find a group to play with.

At 57, she had taken up weaving. She gave all of us one of her projects for Christmas. "Did you hang it up?" she had asked during one of our phone calls. "Yep. I did." *In the hallway...where no one could see it.*

At 58, she had joined a quilting guild.

If I had been home, I might have realized she was changing. She had always told me about her new birthday adventures. I should have seen it coming. While I was off living my life, she was reinventing her own. I suddenly remembered when she went back to college at the age of 42; she had said to us, "I need to find something to do when you don't need me anymore."

I sat down and looked at the picture. I drew a ukulele by her side and called her back.

"So, have you been looking at paint colors for the new house?"

"Just start." The summer after her son graduated from college, this thought goaded **Cindy Cleaver** to go online to see if there was a writing group in the Grand Rapids area.

After graduating from Michigan State University with an English degree (1984), her writing dreams languished during the years of raising children with special needs. She found a local Word Weavers group in July of 2011 and has been meeting with them once or twice a month since. As a result of showing her dream to others on a regular basis, she has been published in *Chicken Soup for The Soul: Raising Kids on The Spectrum* and in *The War Cry* Magazine. She also blogs at annkilter.com about raising children with autism and at odeal59.wordpress.com about journeying out of cynicism. *Another Metamorphosis* is her first foray into fiction since college.

Learning to Stand

By Amy Mills

The canyon walls vibrated with shrieks from the Kakos horde. The demons waited, controlled by the mind of the ancient enemy, Abaddon. Christina stood with the other warriors, facing a wall of bulging eyes and gaping mouths. Black, deformed bodies shifted restlessly as staffs pounded the ground.

Following in her parents footsteps, she had begun preparing to serve the General at a young age. The day she was called to join his army had been a thrilling one. Despite her years of training, Christina shook as she gripped her Makkera blade. The lightweight sword was short with a hooked tip and a point that curved back over her hand. Glancing at the red rock extending above her, she wondered if the Kakos had concealed themselves in the walls. She shook her head to clear her thoughts. *Get a grip!* This wasn't the first time she had fought the enemy, but something was different. The Kakos were bolder, more confident than she had ever experienced. It was as if they knew they would win.

The horde began to advance as an undulating black wave. They ran with a lurching gait, gripping their staffs, white electricity sparking at the tips.

"Stand your ground!" The order came through the

communication network in their helmets. "Fear is their greatest weapon. Do not give in."

Christina adjusted her grip on her blade and focused on the oncoming enemy. Black figures swarmed toward her, and she began fighting for her life. Demons exploded into dust as Christina swung her blade in sweeping circles. The horde never stopped advancing. Dust stung her eyes and left a burnt taste in her mouth. Coughing, she stumbled backward as the Kakos surrounded her. She struck at them wildly, desperately. A Kako sidestepped her swing, bringing his staff up to catch her sword and send it flying. Watching it arc through the air, she backed away from her attacker. He gripped his staff, grinning and licking his lips as the horde behind him shrieked in excitement.

A roar cut through the chaos, and everything paused for a brief moment. The Kakos started cackling and leaping around in excitement. The roar vibrated throughout the canyon again, and a winged beast appeared over the rim. A rider perched on its back, holding reins fixed in the curved beak. Yellow eyes glared down as the beast dived toward the warriors.

Christina leapt back just in time to miss being hit by a glowing staff. Before the beast rider could swing again, a warrior was at her side, dispatching the rider in a cloud of dust.

"Where's your blade?" he shouted.

She looked up and froze. The winged creature was swooping down again. Its yellow eyes locked with hers. Fear coursed through her. Turning, she ran over the uneven ground, slipping on rocks. Suddenly, a bolt of energy shot through her body, and she collapsed. The last thing she saw before blacking out were the yellow eyes coming closer.

*****

Pain was the first thing Christina was conscious of. Her body ached, and her head throbbed. She pressed her hands against her temples and opened her eyes. Trevor was sitting next to the bed, his freckled face breaking into a grin.

"I'm glad you're okay. That was close."

She looked around the infirmary at the full beds. "What happened?"

"The Kakos retreated, but they'll be back. That beast really did a number on us."

"What was it?" She pushed her dark hair out of her face.

Her friend shrugged. "No clue. I've never seen anything like it before."

She groaned and shook her head. "If I hadn't been running, I probably wouldn't have gotten hit. I don't know what happened. I just panicked."

"Anyone would be scared of that thing. You're not the only one who ran from it." He squeezed her shoulder. "Listen, rest for a bit, okay? The General will be in to talk later."

Her mind started to race as Trevor left. This wasn't her first battle, yet she had acted like a coward. The General had every right to be angry with her. In one instant, her training had deserted her. She wasn't fit to be a warrior. Maybe she never had been.

She heard a low voice talking with the nurse, and footsteps approached. Wanting to make a good impression, she tried to spring out of bed and to attention. Unfortunately, her body rebelled. She only succeeded in stumbling awkwardly to her feet. A strong hand gripped her arm, steadying her swaying balance. She looked up into the face of the General. His white hair was clipped short. His tanned and clean-shaven face was serious, but his blue eyes were warm.

"Sit." He guided her back to the bunk.

"Sir, I am so sorry about today," Christina said. "I know I can do better. I'm not sure what happened. I just panicked. If you will give me another chance...."

He held up his hand, interrupting her rambling. "I was watching you today. You fought well…until you lost your blade. Did you forget about your deflector cuff? You can't see the force field it emits, but it will protect you. If you come to a place where you can no longer fight, then stand firm. But never run."

Christina shifted uncomfortably on her bunk. "But, sir." She dropped her gaze to the floor.

"Speak your mind." He urged.

"How can you understand what it's like out there? That… that thing…I just…I didn't know what to do." She looked at the General.

His face softened. "Do you think that I have never been a warrior myself?" He smiled. "I've felt fear. It does not have to control you."

"Sir. That beast. What was it?"

"That was a Morrah. It feeds on fear. When you give in to fear, it grows stronger. The only way to fight it is to stand against it. Nothing can defeat you when you summon the courage to follow my orders." His eyes penetrated her being. The general squeezed her shoulder. "Trust me."

*****

The General's words rang in her mind as she stepped into her suit the next morning. She strapped on her boots, unsure whether she was ready to go into battle again. But she had her orders to suit up. Her hands shook as she fastened her belt. She sheathed her Makkera blade, shaking off the image of it flying from her hands. She slipped on her deflector cuff and picked up her helmet as Trevor poked his freckled face in the door.

"Come on! We've got to get moving."

Christina strapped on her helmet as she rushed into the corridor. Climbing into the vehicles, they heard the voice of the

General in their helmets.

"You have been trained for this. I would not send you out if I didn't think you were ready. You have been given all the tools you need to defeat the Kakos. Only you must remember to use them. Don't back down; we can't let them take the city." His voice softened. "Remember, I will be watching over each of you."

As the vehicles rumbled to the city gates, Christina wondered if he could really keep an eye on her. She wiped the sweat out of her eyes and adjusted her helmet. All too soon the trucks stopped, and they scrambled out.

Warriors were already stationed along the canyon walls that guarded the city. Christina's group spread out and took cover behind rocks and boulders. The horde had been spotted only a mile away and would arrive within minutes.

The shrieking made Christina's head ache long before the demons were spotted. Warriors descended from the walls attacking the horde from all sides. Christina's group advanced from the front. At every swing, Kakos exploded into dust, but they never seemed to decrease. The shrill shrieks continued as Christina swung her blade. Fine ash, hanging in the air like fog, stung her eyes.

A shadow passed overhead, and she looked up to see the Morrah. Its hooked beak, dripping blood, and yellow eyes shot fear through her heart. A Kakos brought his staff down on her sword arm with a crack, sending energy shooting through her. She stumbled backward, dropping her Makkera as she fell. It skittered well out of reach.

The Kakos raised his staff again and brought it down, as if intending to crush her skull. She threw her deflector cuff in front of her, and the air exploded in a white light as the staff contacted the force field. The collision knocked him back, and Christina dove for her blade. She deflected another strike from the staff, but a wave of pain shot through her sword arm when she tried to raise it.

Deflecting two more strikes, she started to back up when she heard a roar. The Morrah was descending on her with talons extended. Panicking, she turned and ran.

"Christina!" The General's voice sounded in her helmet. "Do not run! You are never more vulnerable than when you give in to fear…trust me."

Those words stopped her in her tracks. She turned to face the creature as it swooped down again. Planting her feet, she braced for the impact and raised her deflector over her head. The creature hit her shield at full force, driving her to her knees as white light exploded around her. She stood, blinking as the ground shook, and she saw a large black form writhing in front of her. Suddenly a warrior swung his blade through the neck of the beast, sending dust flying as the horde swept toward them. *Do not run.* The general's words echoed in her mind as Christina faced the swarming mass. Knees weak, she planted her feet and held her deflector steady. Before the horde reached her, she felt a shoulder press against hers.

Trevor grinned down at her. "We're stronger when we work together, right?"

She smiled back. "That's what the General says, and he's never wrong."

They held up their cuffs as another warrior joined Christina on her right. As the force fields contacted one another, the white light started to glow. More warriors joined shoulder to shoulder, and soon a wall of white was shimmering across the canyon. The demons struck the white wall, forcing the warriors back. Facing fear, the warriors raised their blades. Together they took a step forward, and then another, slowly pressing the horde back.

As quickly as it started, the onslaught ceased. The sight of the Kakos retreating back up the canyon raised a shout from the warriors. Pursuing the enemy, they overtook them as the canyon opened out into the desert. The Kakos scattered in all directions, no longer willing to fight. Christina stood, breathing hard amid the cheering and back-slapping. As they returned to the vehicles, she heard words that made it all worth it.

"Well done, my warrior," the General said.

Amy Mills sees herself as a sign language interpreter by profession, a writer and storyteller by nature. She finds that fiction writing is a wonderful way to make a point. She enjoys writing for juvenile and young adults, weaving life truths into fantasy and science fiction.

Amy currently calls Grand Rapids, Michigan her home. The combination of the bustle of the city and quiet of the country is something she finds inspiring!

The Shocking Salvation of Simon Lanore

By Deb Gardner Allard

A light snow fell as Simon Lanore swaggered across Beaumont Street. He winced as sparkling lights on the town Christmas tree winked and blinked in his face. A block further, and he passed a Salvation Army Santa clanging a silver bell and crooning, "Merry Christmas! Merry Christmas!"

Simon growled at the corpulent figure. "Bah! Commercialism at its finest; people hungry for material things. The money would be better spent on bills and…." He stopped, catching himself, and then resumed the tirade. "Gifts never meet expectations, and what does the giver receive…frowns? Disappointment? I despise what Christmas stands for—a savior and love. What is love? And who could possibly save anyone?"

The santa's eyes furrowed at Simon's miserable lament. Simon ignored him and trudged on, until something tugged at his frayed coattail. He whipped around to find a little girl, barely reaching the level of his tarnished belt buckle, peering up at his contorted face. The child, with honey blonde hair and milky brown eyes, smiled.

"Shoo, get out of here! I don't need no kid following me around!"

"Sorry to bother you, sir, but I need money for Momma's medicine."

"You need money for candy. That's what you need, isn't it? Go on. Get outta here!"

"No, sir. My momma is sick. I don't have money for medicine."

"Really, now?" *Just prove your point. March her to the store and see if she's telling the truth.* "Come on," he said.

The little girl in baggy clothes slipped her fingers into his cold, leathery hand. Simon cringed. Years without touching human flesh made the delicate softness of her skin feel foreign. "What are you doing?"

The child dragged him toward an old brick storefront. "I'm showing you the way." A sign heralding Grover's Pharmacy loomed above the threshold of the crumbling shop.

The little girl stopped. "This is it," she said, pointing between a deli and a haberdashery. "This is the medicine place."

"It's called a pharmacy," Simon snarled. "What's your mother's name?"

"It's Madeline Love," the little girl said. "My name is Truly."

"Did you say, 'Trudy'?" Simon corrected.

"No, sir, I said, 'Truly'."

"What kind of dang name is that? I don't have time for nonsense. Let's get your mother's medicine."

Truly led him down an aisle littered with empty boxes and decades-old advertisements. "Momma needs medicine for coughing, sir," she explained.

Simon stumbled to a crowded shelf in the far corner of the store. He snatched the cheapest bottle of cough medicine and flung it on the pharmacy counter before removing a wrinkled ten-dollar bill from his wallet. He tapped fingers on the counter while the pharmacist totaled the purchase. The child stood on tiptoes, watching, her eyes barely peeking above the wooden ledge.

"Here," the business-like lady in white said, handing Simon the package.

"This ain't mine." Simon protested. "The medicine is for *her* mother." He glanced sideways at Truly.

The pharmacist looked to the left, then to the right with arched brows. Simon grumbled under his breath, impatient with the lady's apparent confusion. He grabbed the package and swept Truly from the store in a huff.

"Thank you, sir. I won't bother you again," Truly said. Her scruffy tennis shoes, missing shoestrings, flapped against the sidewalk as she headed away from the store and the bright lights.

"It's dark outside. You can't walk home alone," Simon growled, catching up with her.

Truly smiled then laced her hand in his, once again. "Bothersome child," he mumbled. Try as he might, he couldn't stop the corners of his mouth from curling as he and Truly plodded the pavement.

Before long, a few words of an old hymn from childhood crept into Simon's mind…*Love Lifted Me.* But he didn't have time to savor the memory. A familiar feeling of impending doom struck. A feeling that stimulated a craving for alcohol.

Simon's body released a torrent of sweat, drenching his garb. His hands trembled. He looked to see if Truly noticed, but she showed no reaction. Heat seared his body, scorching nerves along the way. Dreaded worms wiggled up and down his extremities. Shadowy figures floated past the corners of his eyes. "Did you see that?" he shouted, quivering.

"I didn't see anything, sir," the little girl said.

It's coming full force now. Simon released the child's hand and searched his wallet. Three one-dollar bills. *I'd have had enough money if I hadn't given it to her.* "How much further to your house?"

"Oh, it's not a house, sir. We live under the bridge."

"What?"

"You'll see. We'll be there soon."

Truly led Simon another block south, toward the Hope Street Bridge. "There it is!" she shouted, pointing to the large cement structure. "Follow me!"

She descended the brown hillside leading beneath the bridge. Simon lurched down the embankment, unable to steady himself. *I don't need this. I need to get home.* But he couldn't stop himself.

At the bottom of the hill, a barrier of large craggy rocks separated the land from a murky, turbulent river. A large cement cylinder, left behind after completion of the bridge, lay to the left of a steel support column. "Here's my home, sir," Truly said.

A tattered, gray blanket covered the opening of the enormous tube. Simon prepared himself for what lay beyond. *There's probably a homeless woman, fragile and sick, in need of care and compassion. Well, I won't have any of it. I'll show the lady Truly is safe and then leave. I'm not a nurturer. My own kids can testify to that.* Simon lifted a corner of the blanket and peered inside. *What?*

He froze. Nothing could have prepared him for what he saw.

The odor of death stung his nostrils. A skeletal corpse lay with arms crossed over its chest. "Here, Momma," the little girl said. "This nice man paid for your medicine."

Simon fell to his knees. Horror and disbelief clouded his reasoning. *What happened? Did the child believe her mother still existed?*

"She has the *new-monia*," the little girl said, as though answering Simon's unspoken question. "She's all I've got."

Simon doubled over, clutching his face, wailing from the depths of his soul. *Surely the child knows her mother is dead. How does one comfort a child? I can't help her. I can't even help myself. How did I get into this mess?* His shoulders heaved as he sobbed. Cramps seized his gut, and trembling coursed his body. *I have to get out of here. I need vodka. I couldn't handle my wife dying, and I can't handle this!"*

He crawled frantically away from the cylinder, staggering toward the hill. Hand-over-hand, he grasped frozen brown weeds, pulling for momentum to reach the top. At the peak, the last handful gave way, and he floundered to the bottom, missing jagged rocks by inches.

Dazed and confused, Simon redirected his escape. He wrestled up rocky projections to a flat ridge at the highest point of the rock barrier. Then his conscience shattered his heart. *You began drinking when your wife developed cancer, and then you ran off, leaving her to die alone. Even now, when a little girl needs you, all you can think about is escape.*

No! I've never been good at dealing with problems. An urge gripped Simon to throw himself into the churning river—to end it all—his worthless life, the drinking, the nonexistent relationship with his grown sons, whom he couldn't please with all the gifts in the world. They wouldn't forgive him. He didn't deserve forgiveness.

A shadowy figure grew from the center of the river and extended a wispy hand, beckoning Simon to jump. Evil eyes pierced his soul, coaxing him to end it all.

"I can't! I can't!" he cried. "I've had no courage in life, and now, I have no courage in death."

From the corner of his eye, he spotted Truly motioning him back to the cylinder. He hugged rocks as he made his way to the ground, then he teetered behind her to the tomb. Truly disappeared like a wisp of smoke through the blanket. *What the...*

Simon lifted the covering. Only the skeletal corpse of the woman lay beyond. He stumbled, landing face down beside the body. Grasping his head, he wailed, "I did this to my sons! I left them in childhood to tend a dying mother. No money, no support, no compassion. They watched her die, helpless to meet her needs.

I'm a wretched, worthless excuse for a father."

Minutes later, his ability to reason warped into a sea of hallucinations. He curled into a fetal position and raised the collar of his jacket to warm frozen ears. Tremors engulfed his body and gave way to intermittent seizures. Figments of demons with horns and rabid flying creatures tormented him. He could no longer walk, only huddle in a ball, shaking.

Three days later, dehydrated and weak, Simon opened his eyes. The tortuous visions had passed. Somehow, without food and water, he had survived. His clothing hung from his frame, soiled with bodily fluids.

The skeleton lent proof of reality. He sobbed again at the sight. Moments later, he smeared tears from his face with a filthy sleeve, and then wobbled from the tomb, clutching rocks for support and gasping for air. The once turbulent river now flowed gently. The frozen ground had melted, leaving behind muddy soil.

Simon flailed up the sludgy hillside. He waved arms and screamed like a madman trying to hail a taxi. A stunned cab driver felt compelled to escort him to the hospital, but Simon pleaded for return to his apartment.

On his doorstep, Simon opened his wallet before remembering he had given money to the little girl. "I've only got three dollars for fare," he said, offering the bills to the driver.

The driver accepted the money. "Sir, there are thirteen dollars here. You overlooked this wrinkled ten. This will be plenty."

That day, Simon swore off alcohol and summoned the courage to ensure Madeline Love was not forgotten. After regaining strength, he drove to the police station and reported her death.

"How do you know the name of the deceased?" a policeman asked.

"Her daughter told me."

Simon explained the strange occurrence to the officer. The sergeant searched records of missing persons and found none for Madeline Love. "I have an address for her home," he said. "I'll head out there to investigate."

"Can I ride along?" Simon begged.

The policeman consented and they drove to the far side of town. Simon choked as the vehicle pulled into an unpaved driveway in a drug-riddled neighborhood. The broken-down house had been boarded up with a sign on the front proclaiming foreclosure.

Unable to gain entrance, the policeman jimmied a door and stepped inside. Simon followed. The same stench of death as in the cylinder bit their nostrils.

"Come look at this!" the officer hollered.

The skeleton of a young child lay huddled in a corner of the kitchen. Not a morsel of food or furniture lingered in the dwelling.

The officer discovered an opened basement window—the perfect size for a small child to gain entrance. If Truly had entered the home through the tiny space and dropped eight feet to the floor, there wouldn't have been a way to exit. All remaining windows and doors had been boarded.

Simon fell against a row of cabinets in the kitchen and cried. *This could have easily happened to his sons. Truly was left without parents, money, or food. If his sister-in-law had not taken his boys into her home, they might have perished, as well.*

Had Truly been an angel, showing him what could have happened to his own family, and why his boys hated him? Tears flowed as he recalled the sweetness of the child. She hadn't condemned him—only shown him the way.

Simon orchestrated burials for Madeline and her little girl who had taught him about love.

Four weeks passed and Simon remained alcohol-free. When Christmas Day arrived, he phoned his three estranged boys, now grown men, and blubbered, begging forgiveness for the past. The young men invited their father to a family Christmas gathering.

On his way to the appointed home, Simon stopped by the center of town and dropped a bill into the Salvation Army pot. The santa smiled and saluted with two fingers before ringing the bell. "Merry Christmas! Merry Christmas!"

When Simon arrived at his destination, he embraced each son with a tenderness he never believed possible. As they sat around the Christmas tree, adorned with twinkling lights, he handed each one a gift. They scrambled to remove the wrapping paper then sat, speechless.

Inside each small, flat box lay a crisp ten-dollar bill with the words, *truly love,* scrolled in red ink.

"I've learned the true meaning of Christmas," Simon explained in response to their bewilderment. "I should have been here for you kids over the years. I should have been here when your mother died of cancer. I was a coward and a horrible father. I understand now why gifts at Christmas meant nothing to you.

"Believe it or not, love showed me the way. Christmas is not about money or gifts. It is truly about love."

Simon's grown boys gathered for hugs, and Simon freely gave the best gift of all.

Deb Gardner Allard is a retired registered nurse with a bachelor's degree in psychology, who also enjoys writing fiction. Although she writes for all ages, her passion is writing for and about the zany activities of children.

In addition to Word Weavers International, Deb is also a member of the Society of Children's Book Writers and Illustrators of Michigan and the Children's Book Insider Clubhouse. *Izzy and the Real! Truth About Moose Boy,* her first book for 3rd through 5th graders, invites children to determine the difference between teasing and bullying while reading about annoying Moose Boy.

In her free time, Deb enjoys kicking back with kids and taking long walks in the lakeside town of Grand Haven. She invites all to visit her Christian website and weekly blog entitled, *Enjoying Kids,* at www.debgardnerallard.com.

Balthan's Dream

By Gerald Doctor

He wasn't supposed to be here, but the dream had disturbed him enough that he was determined to risk it. From his perch on the side of the mountain, Balthan took one last, yearning look westward across the river valley. He hoped with all his heart that he could one day enter this territory that had become known as, "The Promised Land." *Better head back to camp before I'm missed.*

Having thought about that land so much during the long treks through desert sands and rough mountains, Balthan had sometimes simply called it TPL for short—it was also easier to write in his journal. He wanted so badly to get there.

Someone kept track over the years and claimed their roving itinerary had taken nearly 40 years. Maybe, but who really knew? They had wandered so long that most of them had given up, resigned to trekking through the wilderness indefinitely. "Most of them" meant the older people, of course, but there weren't many left.

Of the original group of adults that had left Egypt *en masse* so abruptly, all but a few had died along the way. Balthan had buried his beloved Miryam several years ago near the edge of the unforgiving and treacherous Malnum Desert during a particularly severe winter. Even the manna had frozen often in the early mornings before some of the late risers could retrieve their share. Painful times, painful memories…

Shivering in the cool desert night air, Balthan roused himself from his reverie to stir the fading embers. He remembered a conversation around a late evening fire when Moses had confided in him about his own disappointment. Because Yahweh, bless His Holy Name, had informed Moses directly to his face, he knew he was destined to die in the wilderness.[1] A glimpse into the promised province, then he'd have to yield tribal leadership to someone else of Yahweh's choosing. The venerable leader tasted the bitterness of the pill, but who could argue with The Almighty?

Now it was Balthan's turn. *I wonder if I'll get there?*

Years earlier the spies had said The Land was extraordinarily rich and productive. Milk, honey, fountains and springs, abundant crops of wheat, grapes, figs and pomegranates, flowing olive oil, rich copper and iron mines. What's not to like?

God had given the people many assurances about the new land. He promised they'd receive their inheritance—new land, new identity, power and authority. They would eat their fill, find rest, defeat their enemies, be exempt from the diseases of Egypt. But the people were afraid.

Balthan worked hard to suppress his disappointment that the tribe rejected Caleb and Joshua's recommendation to grab the land post haste. It was fortunate that Yahweh didn't whack them all on the spot as He threatened to do.

For the people in the wilderness the challenges were enormous. They faced serpents and scorpions, drought, giants, fortified cities, deserts, tough times all around. They often experienced failures, pain and suffering, but God clothed them, fed

---

[1]. Note: In Balthan's time, prophets and other more ordinary mortals heard from God in dreams; Moses and Yahweh chatted directly, face to face (Numbers 12:6-8).

them manna, gave them water from solid rock, and guided their footsteps.

Their wilderness wandering enlarged their vision, created courage in their hearts and allowed them to see God's provision for their needs. Eventually their forced travel would enable them to come to the end of their own strength and to surrender themselves to God, to let go and trust Him.

Trudging along with the camel rope in his left hand and a worn goatskin bag in his right, Balthan had lots of time to muse every day. *Better than tilling that mucky Nile River Delta soil every day with an Egyptian overlord watching my every move. It's a bit boring at times, but no sense complaining. Keep the vision in mind at all times, everybody says. We're going to The Land.*

* * * * *

Balthan had decided it was worth the risk of sneaking away to hike up the nearby mountain in early evening. He had hoped to catch even a brief glimpse of that land the spies had said was not far beyond their encampment. And now that he'd seen it, he knew it was the land they sought, knew it in his bones, knew it in his spirit. This was it!

As he mused about his mountainside escapade, Balthan wondered if the reason it was taking Yahweh so long to allow them to get to The Promised Land was simply because the people weren't ready for it. Weren't *ready* for it? Nearly four decades wandering, sandals getting frayed, garlic and cucumber recipes long forgotten, most of the original crew dead and buried, new kids beginning to assume group leadership roles, and *we're* not ready? What's it going to take?

Maybe the answer was in that dream.

No stranger to dreams, Balthan knew how to approach and uncover the meaning this current one held for him. Yahweh often used dreams to provide answers to Balthan's questions, to guide his footsteps, and to encourage him on the wilderness journey. Despite musing on this new dream throughout the day, however, Balthan had been unable to make sense of it.

Perhaps it was important for other people around him, maybe even for the whole tribe. He'd run it by the Board of Elders first chance he got.

Meanwhile Balthan knew the dream was especially significant for him. It seemed somehow to relate to his own quest for passage into The Land. But how? He ran the dream through his head one more time:

A rabbi is addressing a classroom composed of two distinct groups: vibrant, eager young people, and weary senior citizens. I sit with the older group, most of whom seem to be smart, educated, and sophisticated, but a little jaded. The younger people appear..., well, sort of ordinary, but alert, aware.

The rabbi asks one simple question and then offers a hint: "If you know who you are, you'll know the answer."[2] Almost immediately the young people rise confidently and exit the room. All of us in the older group, confused and uncertain, remain seated.

That was it. No indication of what kind of question the rabbi had posed. Just that mysterious hint requiring an ability to look inside yourself, assess your own character, determine what you believe, what you live for, how you see yourself, and presto, you know the answer.

Suddenly it hit him, the "Aha!" that came when the message

---

[2]. For this profound concept, Balthan and I are indebted to John A. Stroman, *Singing Mary's Song: An Advent Message of Hope and Deliverance* (Upper Room Books: Nashville, TN, 2012), 25.

wrapped up in the symbols of a dream opened up to him. The old people represented the original tribe that escaped Egypt; the young people symbolized the new group born in the wilderness.

To enter the new land the people had to undergo a transformation of their character. Slaves could not possess this new terrain that God said He would give into their hands. It had to be conquered, developed, and defended by a free people.

God had more in mind for His people than they had for themselves. They'd have been content just to escape slavery, but The Almighty wanted to transform how they saw themselves. God desired to turn slaves into free men, then lead them through the wilderness into their own land with a brand new identity. They would need a new name, like their ancestor, Jacob, when he became Israel.

In this sense the younger people enjoyed a huge advantage— they did not carry a slave mentality in their souls. Unlike Balthan's generation who had suffered at the hands of the Egyptians, these fortunate young people who grew up in the wilderness were not saddled with memories of servitude. They were free to live and move and make decisions independent of the chains that dragged down older citizens burdened with a legacy of the taskmaster's whip.

Each person must examine themselves and ask the question: *Am I the author of my life's story, or am I the victim in it*? Tough question to ask someone who'd felt the sting of the Egyptian lash on his back if his pile of mud bricks didn't reach chest high by mid-afternoon. But it demanded an answer.

To claim a space in the new land they'd been promised required an inner transformation. If people left their leek and onion farms on the Nile delta thinking they were slaves (they *were*, after all), there had to be a radical realignment of their inner attitudes, a substantial readjustment inside their souls. If not for individuals, at least collectively for the soul of the whole tribe.

Transformation from slave to free man is not instantaneous —it is a long process. Innumerable hardships and dangers were needed to accomplish this task in the people. Their 40-year adventure was designed so they could discover who they were really meant to become.

Balthan understood this. With a certain amount of regret and, yes, bitterness, he acknowledged his fear that he might never reach his long-held goal. Another group of people, free people who had been transformed by the wilderness experience, would be the ones privileged to enter the new territory. These would be people who had acquired a new name.

The Promised Land is for free people, redeemed by the hand of the Lord, released from slavish obedience to someone else's demands, no longer in bondage to anything. Once the slave has died in the wilderness, a free man is ready to cross the Jordan River.

Is Balthan's dream about to elude him? Or is his dream about to be fulfilled?

Gerald Doctor has successfully navigated the transformative journey from head to heart. After earning an MSEE degree, he experienced a career that spans engineering, technical marketing, freelance writing, and — in an abrupt turn assisted by his dreams — ministry.

Gerald and Judith, his wife of over fifty years, co-founded Kairos Ministries, Inc. in 1999. Together they have ministered in both the USA and Europe, helping people experience the power of God in their lives. Recently they co-authored a book, *Dream Treasure: Learning the Language of Heaven*. The couple currently lives near Grand Rapids, Michigan.

Amid The Transmoglifier's Lenses

By Dan Gray

Just kill me now, solar wind, I silently plead.

Death by water is preferable to burning in the sun, if I can only find the water's edge. I hear my lungs heave for air. *So hot.* My swollen lips crave the life liquid. Not a ripple of the water's waves tickle my sense of direction. No one would miss my bubbles if I fall in.

My eyelids are burned shut. I aimlessly crawl down the beach. I'm shirtless, and my proximity suit flaps on my waist, shredded to my knees. The heat index is off the charts. *Shade. Must find shade.* I blather like a drooling, blind dog hunting for a fire hydrant. The scorching sun feels like midday, but the early-morning crest penetrates through my lids.

At what point does flesh melt?

A static energy knife thrusts its splitting edge through my skull. The stars spring through my fingers and up my arm, striking my heart. Prickling sensations zip through my toes to my chest. A silent scream rips through my soul. My optic nerves are scrambled from the PIDL malfunction. Sun glued, the cortex Parabolic Interactive Differential Lens interface feels like a permanent fixture on my head. The 280g miniaturized head-gear feels like 4 kilos. My PIDL streams a viral headline directly from the news grid into my cerebellum: *Professor Grady Evenstein kills himself by his experimental push ray after several failed attempts.*

What happened? My quantum differential equations are near perfect. Differentials near enough for the slip chaos quotient to be an absolute figure, if there was such a thing.

The water makes no sound, calm as glass. There is no one around for miles. The flat water shows ideal conditions for my perfect calculations. Two-thirds of the world's population had gone underground before the heat wave.

All pain numbing and stuck like putty, I pry my eyelids open. The beach glares prism sharpness and melts like rubberized glass in my hands. The glass blanket of sand on the beach congeals like a mercury bath. My PIDL head-gear reports vitals on the verge of terminal. Warning atmosphere conditions reaching 63 degrees Celsius. Sweat drenches the threads of shorts that remain. My body paints a blood trail down the beach knoll.

A deformed piece of wood lies among the prismatic shore's spectacle. The hollow stump, on its side, struck a miserable pose. Like an old man's hand after a bath, its grooves run deep. Crawling up beside the weathered tree trunk, I rest my back. The drifter feels like a recliner while I soak up the small shadow's relief.

The beach is deserted. No signs of exploding machines from last night, except for remnants of large power cables running up the channel. The pier gathers fog. Sunrays seem to hold the gloomy fog back from spilling into the ocean as if to delay a horror settling on the waters. The searing heat waves will kill me before I get to take the Walk.

I notice an oddity on the pier. A mountain man sits fishing. He's shaded himself with a large-brimmed farmer's hat, his wiry hair spiraling and poking out beneath. The bum probably thinks he has it made, with all the fish floating to the top from the calm, deep channel. Yet I know he'll be dead from radiation poisoning within a day of eating his catch if he doesn't die from dehydration first.

I plan to protect Earth from the deadly solar flares by the impossible task of calculating all ocean surface area and converting its energy into a force field lens. This process will create a hyper-surface capable of solidifying the ozone. I replicated positive results in the lab, sufficient enough to warrant a publication on the push ray's significance.

I rip the pad loose from the back of my PIDL and tap a few more possible equations into the pad. I prepare the data pad for the next thousand-year time capsule and place it in the hollow log. *A treasure that might save the world. 'If you come back and discover my failure, the day is ... '*

"Your lens attempt was not a complete failure." A soothing voice dribbles out of the air like singing tinsel chimes. A tingle springs up my back.

"What? Who is that?" I try to turn around, but my back is stuck to the wood. Pain flashes through my body. The weather-polished wood rips the glued flesh from my back. There is no one around. Only a squeak comes out of my mouth. Curse the pain. A large scorpion scampers up between my legs. Holding my breath, I watch it disappear. The heat boils my energy away. I ease myself back, wincing from the pain as my tender flesh re-congeals with the wood.

I don't see anything out of the ordinary except for the fog fingers stretching across the bay line and the lone, crazy-haired fisherman.

"88.997 squared traplic conversion over the local time speed normalcy differentials..." the voice oozes. Translating, "...You caused a wave differential in our dimensional plaining."

"Who's talking?" I ask again, thinking I am on the edge of insanity. Then I see a glass-like life form step into focus from a forming oval ripple in the air. Its edges are smooth, and there is a slight wave of a jiggle to the creature.

"I am A'lob," the liquid voice said, "a lens crafter. Your lens disturbance has caused local dimensions to transduce simultaneously, viewers and refractor alike.

"What's going on?" A horizontal ripple forms in front of me like a stone tossed in a pond. A faint chorus of singing bowls accompany the evaporating ocean. I feel unsure with my hazy vision, but I reach out and poke the forming ripple. "My push ray…did it work?"

"Can you feel it? The lens you've created?"

I reach out and dab a few more ripples in the air with heavy arms. "Traplic conversion? Dimensional plaining? I've never heard of these computational theories before."

"Truth is not a theory. This truth I speak of appears to be theory to you. You refuse to see the truth or have not proven to yourself that your theoretical discovery is real. Because of this, you will not know the truth until you accept it…truth is truth no matter how you attempt to twist it."

A'lob motions over the scene before us. "Can you see the lenses before you? Your lens disturbance is causing local dimensions to transduce simultaneously, viewers and refractor alike."

Creepy fog fingers slither along the ridge toward me. A dark vision floats near, just out of sight. It whispers, "Take the walk. Flesh goes where it came. The water is fine. Take the walk."

"In the name of The Presence," A'lob's liquid voice demands, "Foglimator be gone. In this plane you will recognize the authority of His name – Jesus Christ. You must leave at once."

If this creature has been around since the dawn of time and proclaims by this name, perhaps this person, Jesus, is real.

I cough. Cool vapor exits. *This is strange.* My nose is also bleeding. I'm not a nose bleeder, even when death had nearly snatched me in the lab back when I was exposed to deadly radiation. *Thank the ghosts of Redlady.* I had gulped the formulated protection pill down in time to rid myself of the radiation and to be neutralized.

Another shadow figure creeps up behind me just beyond perceptive focus and introduces himself. I am mystically frightened by his presence, unlike A'lob. The creature doesn't notice A'lob's presence at first.

"I Am...has come to take you," the dark mist says. My heart jumps, producing highly dangerous pressures in my chest.

"Who are you?" I ask. The gloomy creature suddenly shutters to the presence of A'lob.

"I...am the translucifier, Darkatot."

"Go away! He does not yet belong to you," A'lob says.

Darkatot growls. "Not yet."

A'lob explains to me, "This creature is from the separate realm."

"Show me the way. That's where I'm headed," I say to Darkatot. Things can't get any weirder.

"No," A'lob says, glancing towards the pier. "You cannot go. You are not ready."

The fisherman gets up from his spot and starts towards us. Darkatot fades back over the knoll as the fisherman walks closer. My perception of time slows even more.

"Are you an alien?" I didn't say angels, because I don't believe in angels. Angels are for children. To believe in angels and God would just be illogical.

"No, we are not aliens or angels, not in the sense you believe. We are native to your plane. However, my kind are normally invisible and unfamiliar to your visual spectrum. Our existence has been spoken as a step below your existence, yet it seems as though we've been graced to retain our first knowledge from cycle one. We are trans-dimensional entities in service of The Presence."

"Who...what is this Presence?" I ask A'lob.

"He is the Creator of all existence."

"Who is the Creator? Aliens or beings from ancient myths?" I wonder aloud. "String theory places the Big Bang thirty odd billion years ago."

"I know of the concept that you think you know. We view this vibration as The Presence's voice. The result is His creation. On the first cycle of our existence, we observed all that is said that is, not in billion cycles, yet as His Word says. To us, the term 'cycles' transpire as more than just the concept of time. Time is a temporary limitation to a physical being of your kind.

"You talk of many wars and historic events, yet your people fail to believe. The Presence has many names, though none of those you think are His name. He is the I Am Who I Am. He is The Prime Mover. Without His Presence, or the essence of His Love, the energy of matter would not hold together."

I look around, trying to grasp at least part of what he says. Nothing sticks to my overwrought senses. "Is this where you live?" I ask.

A'lob's long pause makes me question whether I can trust this being.

I try again. "What do you want from me?"

"This is a mission of first contact," A'lob says finally.

I shield my eyes from the blinding sun rays and discover he isn't casting a shadow. Taking notice of my situation, he asks, "Today seems to be a particular vibrant day, don't you think?"

I grunt. "Where do you live if you consider this weather, 'a particularly vibrant day?' How can you be so cheerful? I'm melting here!"

"In our rest states, we reside here, in a space rarely seen by human eyes," A'lob says. His fluid gesture wobbles towards the vast bright space superimposing over the ocean.

I shake my head, trying to make sense of it all. "What do you do here?"

"I've been promoted to lens crafter and lens operator. We provide travel lenses for the divine transversal kind. So while your experiment lacks the pertinent energy, the simultaneous spectral allows us to transverse with each other for the first time. This is our secondary purpose."

"What is your primary purpose?"

"To worship The Presence. The Prime Mover. The Transmoglifier."

"Transwhatsit?"

"Transmoglifier; The One who creates, to create or transform a wave into energy and matter," A'lob explains. "Matter, in your case, has been Fogified into a ripple of dark spectral. The Transmoglifier is infinitesimally smaller than our physical containers, yet He is unimaginably larger than thought can calculate. He is not bound by time or by any physical or nonphysical realm or by any other existence one might split into. He cannot be bound and has no beginning, no ending."

"Everything has a beginning. I am a scientist. Not a meta-physicist. But I know everything is made up of energy."

"You are correct when you say everything *has* energy. Yet, in the sense of a corporeal existence and any other frame of mind, there is more than an existence of energy. We first came out of goo, not the single-cell organism you're thinking of. We came from the same dust of this earth that you did. Can you feel it among your lower digits?"

I look down at my wiggling feet sunken in the translucent sand, neither crystallized nor quite solid. *This is not natural.*

"The Presence," A'lob continues, "had formed your being with His life breath. I was there – the first one cycle – as His Presence modified dirt into your king. The First One – he was called Adam.

"The First One's refractors performed perfectly aligned. Elegant spectral emanated from him. The Foglimator twisted the

First One and his cyclomeiosis phase mix element of his being's spectral waves. One of the One's states was not to be modified. Then the First One refracted bent waves. The rippling waves are still being modified in this existence cycle. Refractors of the Foglimator has manipulated the First One's genetic makeup that diluted the original design. This action forced The Presence to gather the pure Ones and destroy the rest of the Foglimator's bent waves."

"So you're saying this person appeared out of mud before your eyes or from your refractors? Then this evil Foggy guy," I become aware of how chilling this fog behind me feels, "he deceived this person's wife who came from him. The children of Mr. Foggy diluted the first person's genetic code so badly that the Big Guy started over. I get it. You're talking about Adam and Eve, then about Noah and the flood." I try to move, but I'm still glued to the wood. *I'll roast before this creature finishes his story.*

A tone hits me like a monastery bell. Ripples spread across the expanse. A space of ephemeral delight flattens out before me and superimposes over my vast ocean view. I feel total peace. The crystal ocean's brilliant colors radiate a million times sharper than hyper HD displays. I am free from my wooden shackle. "Am I in the water?"

"No, you are sitting on the beach. Moments have shortened."

"Are you telling me you can stretch time?" A vast matrix room permeates before me, with translucent colors I've never seen before.

"Yes. This is a section of the realm where we rest our machines."

"You call all of these machines? Or are they lenses?"

"Our kinds are like lenses."

"They look more like weird jellyfish and octopus morphed together, their insides replaced with lava lamp liquid."

I realize the fisherman is standing over me. Chills run down my body. He offers his hand. I take it, and with no effort he gently pulls me to my feet. No skin remains on the wood. I wipe my hands together and notice the blood chips are gone.

A'lob acknowledges him in a low, reverent bend. "Litocore is your escort," he says.

I stand with no pain. I stretch my neck to see the pier. *Was this the same man I saw earlier?* This man has a fantastically white beard. Stars spark in his eyes. His earlier wholly wooly garments appear as a polished red rust color. With no word, he motions toward the ocean. I feel peace, not fear of death. As we stroll toward one of A'lob's machines, I glance back to notice the cross shape of the driftwood.

I hear a voice say to me, "Your color has Transmoglified. You are ready to meet the Transmoglifier."

First as a reader and then as a writer, **Dan Gray** has enjoyed exploring the myriad twists and turns of the science fiction world for a few years now. A loyal Word Weavers member, he strives to offer concrete critique to other members while accepting it graciously on his own work.

In addition to his passion for writing, Dan also loves music. He counts himself blessed to have access to a studio loft. Here he can write, practice, and record in a comfortable and well-equipped setting. You might also find him performing on his trombone with a local band, whose specialty is the big band sound.

Dan currently works for a hearing wellness manufacturing company and enjoys his home in Hart.

Stripped Bare

By Anna Moore Bradfield

I had no idea how they ever passed their classes. With mid-year finals looming, I knew I would be studying. My roommates would be partying.

They had all promised to binge at a friend's tonight. I had even bribed them with brew money so that I could study in peace. But here they were, lounging like lizards in the late-day sun as it filtered through the apartment's windows. They'd spent my money all right, as evidenced by the open cans on every table, the faint smell of hops and wheat mingling with the smoke from their lit cigarettes.

The music hadn't started. The guests hadn't arrived. But it wouldn't be long. "Kyle, you won't even know we're here," one of them said. Right. I'd heard that before.

My semester grades hinged on the results of tomorrow's finals. For a split second, I considered running over to the library. I'd heard they would be open late tonight, and the one on campus was only about a half-mile away.

I don't know why, but the thought of doing something as simple as changing my routine in this way rubbed me wrong. Since I paid rent – since I usually helped at least one of *them* pay rent every month – I felt like I had earned the right to study in my own room. I don't know. A therapist would probably say I had *control* issues. Whatever. It worked for me.

I closed off my room, donned a pair of ear buds, and prayed for the best. Within minutes, the walls pulsed with bass undertones from the old, oversized stereo in the living room.

Throughout the evening, I would open my door to catch the eye of one of my roommates. He'd give a knowing nod and announce to the ever-growing throng, "Hey, guys. Keep it down. Our roommate's studying." The quiet never lasted long, and my vain efforts felt more frustrating at every turn.

When I couldn't take it anymore, I threw my door wide and flew to the stereo, pulling the cord out of the wall. Amid violent protests, I yelled, "Okay, you guys. How many times do I have to say it? I need to study. You guys know that. You…oh! Just forget it." I stomped to my room, hoping I'd made a lasting impact. Knowing better.

Checking my bedside clock, I sighed: 1:17 a.m. If I didn't get to bed, I'd sleep through the tests altogether. I couldn't afford that.

Undressing, I folded my clothes across a chair, the same way I had done for as long as I could remember. The organization of it all – jeans, shirt, socks, boxers, belt – soothed me. Besides, it would help in those times when I needed to dress quickly. I know…*control* issues.

Flopping into bed, I drifted with the walls' pulse.

Dad had been a drinker. I remembered the fights it caused growing up. He could go from melancholy to madman faster than anyone I had ever seen. He wasn't often home before I fell asleep, but he'd wake me on a whim as he opened the front door of our too-small house. "Look at this pigsty!" he'd yell from downstairs. "Kyle! Get dressed. You have work to do."

I could dress in my sleep, I was so often awakened like this in the middle of the night. My room had been something I could control, and I'd kept it pin-clean. But Dad could always find something around the house for me to do.

"Rake the leaves!

"Clean out the refrigerator!

"Scrub the mopboards!"

The day he left, seven years ago now, was both the best and the worst of my life.

From that moment, I had decided who the man of the house would be. If I studied hard and stayed sober, I figured I could really make something of myself. I'd make my mom and sister proud, something Dad had never been able to do, at least as far as I could tell. Did Mom ever hear from him? She never said. Oh, well. It didn't matter. We were better off without him.

* * * * *

I thought I was dreaming. In the utter blackness of my room, somebody snickered and yanked my covers back before I could move. Another idiot squealed and hooted near the bedroom door. I was not in a laughing mood. No, my mood proved a little fouler.

I had no idea how many there were, let alone *who* they were. Could've been anybody, as many as had crossed our apartment's threshold that night. Did my roommates know that these yahoos were here? Had they allowed it? *Were they a part of it?* Did they think this was funny or something? They were about to find out just how funny I thought this whole thing was.

Kicking. Throwing punches. Lunging. Giggles, but not from me. The occasional "Owww!" whining at me through the darkness further bolstered my resolve.

For awhile I thought I was gaining steam, actually overpowering them. That didn't last long. Eventually they pinned my arms back, and I couldn't get free. For some reason, whatever they threw over my head caused them to bust out with laughter. Their good time at my expense infuriated me, but there was really nothing I could do once they bound my wrists and began dragging me toward the front door.

"You need to study, bro," someone said. "We're making that possible." Though I railed, they threw me into a car and crowded in around me. The music blared, drowning my objections as we drove to points unknown. When we stopped, they hauled me out onto the brick-hard ground. My bare feet combed the grass, as stiff as hay. I struggled to stand as the car took off, spitting earth back at me.

Silence. Cold. Panic.

C'mon. Get it together. Think.

I flung my upper torso like a bull until the cloth — my boxers — dropped to the ground. Staring down in disbelief, I thought, *What'd you expect? You sleep in the nude, remember? Did you think they'd dress you?*

I shook my head, straining to re-focus. Sweat broke out, indiscriminate of flanks or forehead, as I worked to free my hands. *Nice*, I thought, wincing at the chafing abuse my wrists were undergoing in the process. These guys had used my own belt as the restraint.

I donned my boxers and discovered that I had been thrown on the library's front lawn. Not the one on campus but the one in town. I figured I was about three miles from the apartment. My scant apparel stopped any further thoughts of flagging a car. I'd run for it, I decided.

The pebbles and cement shocked my feet, but my five-miles-a-day, five-day-a-week running schedule paid off. Before I knew it, I was sprinting up the apartment's stairs to the door that read "303."

I jiggled the knob. *They picked tonight to lock the door?* I had hounded the guys about this all year, to no avail. Now my own words haunted me. I knocked and listened, pounded and yelled. No one stirred.

I banged on other doors. Other halls. Other floors. "Please! I need help!"

One of the neighbors, the lady in 107, opened her door. "Get outta here, you drunk! Go on, before I call the cops!"

"I'm not a drunk!" I protested as she slammed the door in my face. Drunk – the word enraged me. That name described my dad, but I would never, *ever* be him or anything like him.

"Call the cops! C'mon!" I pounded for what seemed like hours but inspired no further response.

I kicked the door and slumped to the stone floor. A flickering sign about a quarter-mile away caught my eye. *Doughnuts! Aren't those places open 24 hours?* The need for warmth took precedence over my pride, my pain, and my fatigue. I ran.

The abandoned lot – lines all but rubbed away – and the dark interior were lost on me until I found the door locked. I stared at the sign. "We've moved! Visit us at…"

I can't believe I'm going to die at the door of a doughnut shop.

My feet screamed, both from the cold and from the beating they'd taken on the unforgiving pavement, but another light caught my eye.

Bus stop. It's unheated, but at least it's shelter. Maybe I'll get lucky with a bus.

Staggering up, my eyes fell to the benches. My temperature dropped 10 degrees just thinking about sitting on metal, but I was exhausted. I had to rest.

Newspapers would serve as a rug. Sitting on them and pulling my knees in tight, I rested my back against a bench.

Between fantasies of blankets and bonfires, I cursed my roommates. I cursed the lady who wouldn't call the cops. I cursed the bus that never came.

I cursed my dad. I felt like he'd left me all over again.

I wished I could escape. If I could get drunk, I wouldn't care about the cold. I wouldn't care about finals, classes, or plans. I wouldn't care about anything. I could just numb myself and die.

* * * * *

"Hey, buddy. Are you with me? Here. Take a nip."

I roused. A guy with both scraggly beard and attire sat beside me. *Homeless guy,* I thought. But who was I to judge? I accepted the flask, desperate for any feeling of warmth. The whisky felt like fire as I swallowed, but I relished it.

Homeless Guy chuckled. "Looks like you left home without bus fare."

"And then some," I said, nodding my appreciation for this show of hospitality.

"Let's warm you up," he said as he helped me stand. Removing his long, outer coat, he wrapped me in it. I cringed, pushing stiffened arms through the ratty but oh-so-warm sleeves, while he buttoned the front. Retrieving a knit cap from the front pocket, he pulled it over my ears.

"You need your coat, Old Man."

"Oh, stop. I planned ahead. I got layers." Homeless Guy patted his puffed chest. "Flannel, thermal, fleece…you name it, I'm wearing it." I looked him over as he kicked his boots off. I'd thought him a big man. Now I realized his bulk came from the layers.

"Your coat's one thing, but I can't take your boots."

"These? Oh, they wouldn't fit those canoes you call feet. No, I'm trying to tap my sock stash." He removed four from each foot with socks to spare. He dressed my feet with two each, reserving the others for gloves. The sweats he handed me were too short, but the socks filled the gap.

"Name's George," he said, waving away my repeated protests. "Who're you?"

"Kyle."

George nodded. "That's my son's name. About your age, too."

My heart beat faster. His face reddened. His eyes seemed familiar, but they kept darting from side to side. But my dad's name wasn't George. *Did this guy fake his name to throw me off?*

George told me about the family he lost to alcoholism: the little girl he called Emily, the wife whom he said had always been out of his league, and Kyle.

"Yep, I rode him hard. Too hard, I imagine. I just loved him. I was so proud of him…wanted so much more for him than I could ever give."

George took a swig and continued, staring off into the distance. "Smart kid. Wouldn't doubt that he found his way into a college like this one here in town."

It was my turn for a swig. "Why'd you leave?"

"Figured they were better off without me. I left with a full flask and an empty pocket. I miss 'em, though. I wonder if they ever think of me."

"They do. Trust me."

"Fondly, do you think?"

I shrugged.

As we talked, I watched George transform. He hoped again, his eyes full of life. He longed again, to be something more than he'd been before.

When the bus stopped, I waved it on. I couldn't leave George. He rooted me to this spot.

I would never know if I sat with my dad that morning. It didn't matter anymore, not really.

In the last hours, I'd been stripped bare of any control. I'd known pain. I'd known shame. I'd known anger. But I'd known forgiveness, too.

I had come to grips with my past, and George helped me do that. Huh. I guess I went through a transformation of my own.

Anna Moore Bradfield has been spinning tales, exaggerating the truth, and flat-out lying almost as long as she could talk. Nowadays, though, she calls it fiction.

Anna's inspiration for her short story evolved from a real-life event she had heard about. It seems a nude man had been found in a very unlikely outdoor space, blue but alive, early one cold Michigan morning. Anna couldn't help wondering what put the guy there. Was this a prank that went awry? Was the guy drunk or high? Had he simply forgotten where he put his pants? What was the story behind the story? *Stripped Bare* helped her resolve those questions.

Anna has enjoyed a productive and enriching career in the field of Human Resources. She currently works in training and development, leading culture change efforts through curriculum creation and facilitation. She is also a writer of both children's stories and adult fiction. In addition to being a loyal member of Word Weavers, the Christian Writer's Guild, and American Christian Fiction Writers, she has published devotionals with *The Secret Place* and articles with the *West Michigan Christian News*. She is also a regular columnist for the *Norton-Lakeshore Examiner*. Visit her website at www.AnnaMooreBradfield.com.

More Than Meets the Eye

By Eugene K. Koon

Mark woke in a daze. He watched his wife Sue drag herself out of the bedroom. He followed shortly. After being married for ten years, they knew each other's routines all too well. Most days they could go about their business without talking. They weren't unhappy, just comfortable. They knew one another's thoughts. Could finish one another's sentences.

Today, however, something was different. Mark sensed a strange feeling hanging over their home as they ate breakfast. It felt like a monster hid in the shadows.

Sue stepped over to the picture window and peered into the street. Loud, boisterous voices funneled through, despite the triple panes.

"Something's going on out there."

"Like what?"

"I don't know. Everyone's heading down the road."

"Can you see where they're all going?"

Sue craned her head in the window. "No, but I hear some kind of music playing."

Mark stepped next to his wife to see what she saw. "Come on. Let's go and check it out."

Once outside and near the street, a strong compulsion to follow the crowd took over. Mark shook his head and lightly tapped his ear. He turned to Sue and said, "I have repetitive audial cogesis."

"Well, don't get any on me."

"I mean, I have an earworm."

"That sounds disgusting." Sue rolled her eyes and shook her head. A little smile crept over her lips, though she tried to suppress it.

"I have a song stuck, looping over and over in my head."

"What's the song?"

"The theme to the old Transformer's cartoon. You know – 'Transformers: More Than Meets the Eye.'"

"You're weird."

"You knew that when you married me. Besides, how do you think I feel? I just want to get rid of this song in my head."

They walked on in silence, not noticing the crowd that had grown around them. The street widened and became smoother, going on as far as the eye could see. Ahead, they could hear the music playing.

Mark said, "What does that sound like to you?"

"Like a sad, broken-down carnival," Sue said.

"Yeah, like a calliope that needs a tune up."

To their left, a woman standing just off the road caught their eye.

"Turn around," she yelled. "There's danger ahead."

Some people in the mob ignored the warnings, waving her off as a wacko. Others mocked her. Mark and Sue didn't give her a second thought as they moved on.

"I don't see any danger," someone yelled from the mob.

"The road is in perfect condition."

"You're crazy, lady."

The crowd cheered in agreement.

Mark laughed at the comments of the crowd.

"I feel a little sorry for her," Sue said.

The ever-growing crowd moved forward, jostling Mark and Sue into the middle of the street. As they moved ahead, bumping and crowding occurred without regard to anyone around them. Several people raced through, knocking others aside, trying to get to the front of the line. A chain reaction of unruliness followed, with fighting breaking out. Mark and Sue dodged out of the way to avoid getting involved.

Another woman, standing next to a man holding a sign, began gesturing to everyone. The sign read, "The end is near."

"Where have I seen that before?" Mark mocked.

"You must go back! It isn't safe." The woman had her hands cupped around her mouth.

"They're certainly relentless," Sue remarked.

"It's kind of bizarre," Mark said. He reached over and took hold of Sue's hand. It was more of a defensive move than one of reassurance or love, but it felt good. The mob carried the couple farther down the street.

The woman on the side of the widening road moved along with them, gesturing, urging and pleading for them to turn back. A man stepped next to her, his face etched with fear and concern for the crowd.

"Please, listen to me! There's danger up ahead," the woman kept yelling.

"You must turn back now." The man pointed in the opposite direction of the moving mass.

This time the mob not only hurled insults, but they also started throwing things. Several rocks barely missed them. One didn't. The rock opened a gash on the woman's right cheek. The crowd pointed, cheering with delight as they marched onward. The man tended to the woman's bleeding cheek as she continued warning the crowd.

"I still have that song stuck in my head – 'Transformers: More Than Meets the Eye,'" Mark said, ignoring the warnings.

"How did you ever get that in your head?"

"I have no idea. It was there when I woke up. It's not like I've watched the cartoon recently."

The road suddenly tilted, as if it had buckled under intense heat. A slippery film, like a newly waxed floor, covered it. People started to slide. Some enjoyed the feeling and moved their feet as if ice skating. Some treated it like they had just reached the apex of a roller coaster. Older adults moved more cautiously as a cat might move while stalking its prey. Oddly, no one seemed to be in fear.

Mark and Sue slid along with everyone else. With the road continuing to fill, there was nowhere else to go but with the flow. Slowing down, stopping, or turning around might get them crushed by the throngs of souls now picking up speed.

More people stood on the sides of the roads giving out warnings.

That same woman shouted at them again. "Stop now."

"Turn back," said the man with the sign.

"There's danger coming soon," another man added.

"It's not too late," the woman said, as if it was her last chance to get the words out.

"They just will *not* give up," Sue said.

"I have to admit, I'm beginning to wonder about our decision to get on this road in the first place."

"You believe what they're saying?"

"Not entirely. It's the way everything around us is changing. To be honest, the people on the side of the road are pretty believable. Just look at their faces." Mark pointed at the woman, among others. "They look normal, just like us."

"You think we're normal?" Sue teased. "So what do you want to do?"

"I guess it wouldn't hurt to talk to them…see what the

danger is they keep yelling about."

"Okay, but how are we going to get over there?"

"Come on." Mark tightened his grip on Sue's hand as they turned around. They faced a mob of people who seemed not to care a thing about who might be in front of them. Mark and Sue were jostled and jolted as the river of people rushed around them.

Sue noted the glazed, haunted look in their eyes. "They look like we did when we woke up this morning."

Other people were trying to make their way to the side of the road as well, the man directly in front of them, for one. Mark reached out with his free hand and took hold of his jacket. The man looked back and nodded. Together they began to angle their way over to the side. The going was made more difficult with the slick surface of the street and the mass of people pushing them farther down the road.

"Now I know how salmon feel," Mark said to Sue.

"Come on, you can make it," urged the woman, now with a bandage on her face.

"Hurry, there isn't much time." A man who stood on the side held his hand out.

Others had made it to the street's edge. They now waved their arms, pleading with others to join them.

The street crowd threw rocks and bottles at those standing on the side, all the while continuing their insults.

"Shut up, lady," screamed an unknown man.

"Maybe you should step out here with us," a woman yelled. Everyone whooped and hollered at this comment.

Mark and Sue neared the curb. The crush of people increased as the road sloped to an even steeper angle and grew slicker.

"Take my hand!" A man on the side of the road strained toward the man Mark held on to. Mark's grip on Sue's hand grew tighter. Sue had joined hands with a woman behind her who also held the hand of someone else. The chain reached far into the depths of the flowing river of people.

The man in the front stepped off the road and pulled Mark up, with Sue right behind him. The moment they stepped off, Mark and Sue could clearly see what was further down. They stood in shock as terror filled their faces.

The road turned remarkably steeper and slicker, as if someone had covered the surface with ice. Hordes of people just slid off the end and were gone. No one stopped going forward. The music now sounded like a horror film soundtrack.

Snapping out of the shock, Mark and Sue stepped back to the edge of the road. They started warning the people in the street.

"You're going to die if you don't get off the road!" Mark yelled, reaching out to anyone willing to take his hand.

"Please, let us help you," Sue cried, standing next to Mark.

Several people began to heed the warning, making their way to the side.

Sue turned to the woman next to her. "I'm so sorry I didn't take your warning earlier. I honestly thought you were crazy." They embraced as long lost friends might do. "I'm just glad you didn't give up."

Another man came up from behind. His placid face conveyed peace beyond all understanding. "Follow me," he said, his voice calm and assuring. It was as if his invitation was meant especially for Mark and Sue.

They left the road's edge, while the woman next to them went back to her warnings. They followed the man several paces before Mark looked back at the street. Sue looked back, too.

Mark saw it now – the glazed yet empty eyes that Sue had mentioned earlier. The people were just going with the flow.

"Like lambs to the slaughter," she whispered, as if reading his thoughts. Mark squeezed her hand gently.

They turned back toward the path, as narrow as the width of their feet, while their guide led them on. Rocks and holes, twists and turns, and steep cliffs made the way treacherous. Mark gripped Sue's hand, both for assurance that she was still there and for balance.

"Where are we going?" Mark asked.

Their guide just kept walking.

"Mark, I'm getting scared. I think I want to go back to the road – try to get more people to the side."

"Let's just give it a little more time. This guy asked us to come with him for a reason. If it doesn't get better, we can always turn back around." They kept moving up the path, holding hands with their backs scraping the side of the hill. Their guide never looked back. They couldn't see more than a step ahead.

Nearly at the top now, Mark stopped to catch his breath. The climb had taken all of his strength. Panting, Sue stood next to him. Perspiration drenched their shirts.

From this vantage point, they could look back down toward the road and see its full path. They could only shake their heads. No order. Only chaos, as the people kept pushing forward.

The end of the road was like a giant waterslide. Bodies dropped from it and into a waiting pit.

"How come the pit isn't filling up?" Sue asked. "There are so many people falling in."

"I'm not really sure. But look at what's happening, about where we got off." Mark pointed toward the line of people trying to reach the side. It had grown significantly from when they had been there. Scores of people just like them were stepping off the street now. They began to follow the path Mark and Sue had just climbed.

The two crested the hill. The sight before them caused them to gasp in unison. A serene lake was surrounded by those who had gone before them. The peace they read on those faces revealed something they couldn't explain.

Mark looked Sue in the eyes. "Still want to go back to that

road?"

"This looks pretty good to me."

"Hey," Mark said, patting her on the shoulder, "I just noticed that song is no longer stuck in my head."

He looked back down the path they took and found their guide leading another couple.

"How did he get back down so fast?"

Sue looked to see where Mark pointed. "That's easy. He's the Son of God."

Smiling, they stepped over the summit of the hill and entered the peaceful setting.

Eugene M. Koon began writing songs while attending the Baptist Bible College in Springfield, Missouri, where he studied Church Music. During his years there he started writing short stories. It wasn't until after his graduation in 1989 that he started with the notion of writing a book. This was accomplished in the mid-1990s. Since this time, he has written two novels and is currently working on the third. He has two published pieces: the lyrics to his song *Hard to Say Good-bye* made a 1999 anthology (*On the Road*) produced by the Association of Songwriters and Lyricists. The second piece is an article recently published in the spring/summer 2013 edition of Halo Magazine. He is currently working towards starting his blog.

A Visit to Jerusalem

By Delbert Teachout

Ten-year-old Timothy squeezed the hand of his mother
Eunice as he looked in terror at the nightmare in front of him. He
came to Jerusalem with his parents during the Passover expecting
excitement and celebrations, but his experience was far from
exciting. His mother tried to hold her other hand over his eyes.
Though he wanted her protection, he kept wiggling free so he
could see.

An unruly mob had dragged a man from the city by his feet.
They stopped in front of Timothy as his family reached the edge of
the town. The man trying to wrestle himself free shouted about
Abraham and Moses, accusing the men who were dragging him.

"Was there ever a prophet," he cried, "that your fathers did
not persecute? Moses predicted a Righteous One would come, and
you have even killed him!"

The crowd erupted with rage. Yelling at the top of their
voices, they began mocking him and throwing stones at him.
Through the tumult, Timothy heard the man yell, "I see the Son of
Man standing at the right hand of God." A large rock struck his
face. Blood splattered onto Timothy's feet.

The crowd cheered and chanted, "Death to the blasphemer!"
More stones hit him, striking him everywhere, raising large welts

all over his body. The crowd raged on even when he fell and hit his head on the ground. No one in the crowd listened to him. But through all the noise Timothy heard the man cry out, "Lord, do not hold this sin against them." Then he fell silent.

The crowd became a frenzied mob. The man lay silent. Some of the crowd picked up the man who had thrown the fatal stone and carried him on their shoulders in a triumphant procession. The man lay silent. The wild chanting continued. The man lay silent. Timothy looked around and saw an important-looking man – his father said he was a Pharisee – holding the coats of those who threw the stones. The Pharisee's satisfied smile indicated his approval. The man who lay silent must have deserved to die.

Timothy saw tears flowing down his mother's face. He watched as she put her head on his father's chest and wept. Timothy did not understand. Who was the man they stoned? Why did they kill him? Who were Abraham and Moses? Who was the man holding the coats? Why was Mother crying?

"I did not come to Jerusalem so my son could watch a man be stoned to death," she sobbed.

Timothy wished he had stayed in Lystra with his grandmother Lois. He could have stayed there, but he had begged to be part of the great family adventure. He had always been too young to come before, but this year he came so he could see Jerusalem for the first time. He learned that Jerusalem was filled with lots of angry people.

Everyone argued about someone named Jesus. Some said he was of God. Some said he was of the devil. Some said he was only a man. Timothy wondered why everyone was so angry.

Back in Lystra, people argued about things, too – how much a goat costs, who the best carpenter is – but nobody died by stoning.

Timothy tugged at his father's tunic. "Father, can we go home?"

"We will leave today. I am sorry you saw this."

People stopped celebrating and began screaming when Roman soldiers arrived at the scene. The crowd ran in every direction. Soldiers cursed Jews. Jews cursed soldiers. Everyone cursed followers of The Way. Hatred. Hatred everywhere. When the soldiers came upon the dead man, those who lingered near identified him as Stephen, one of the disciples of Jesus.

"Jesus? That explains it! How could someone dead for five years continue causing trouble in Jerusalem? Was this man for or against him?" The captain of the guard asked no one in particular. "Someone take him out and bury him."

Timothy wondered what happened to the man holding the coats.

The soldiers caught one man who did not run. They ripped off his tunic and struck his back with a whip. Timothy tried to shout that they had the wrong man, but his father slapped his hand over Timothy's mouth. "These men are not like the Roman soldiers in our town. These men hate everyone.

"Remain silent. If we say anything, they will arrest us."

Timothy thought Passover should have been a time of celebration, a time of merriment. But with all the trouble he had seen – his mother crying, his father frightened – Timothy vowed he would never come to Jerusalem again.

As they continued into Jerusalem, Timothy could see smoke rising high above the city. Someone said that followers of Jesus lived in the inn near the Pool of Siloam so some of the crowd had set it on fire. Someone else said that the hatred for Christ-followers that erupted into the stoning of Stephen whetted the appetites of the Pharisees. The priests demanded that every follower of the Way be driven from town, imprisoned, or killed. Timothy looked on as crowds invaded homes, forcing people to leave with no provisions. On a hill they called Golgotha, Timothy saw a cross burning. He knew he would never forget that sight.

Timothy's family arrived at the inn where they had made arrangements to stay; it had not been torched. Still, everyone seemed to be leaving the inn. Timothy's father told the innkeeper they would not need the room after all. They left town, hoping to make Damascus by nightfall. His father said, "If anyone asks, we do not know Stephen, Jesus, or any of his disciples."

The little family traveled in silence. Eunice and Timothy rode on one donkey, and his father rode on the other.

The boy felt buried in his thoughts and fears, horrified that he had come to Jerusalem. Eunice told him that she remembered leaving Jerusalem in haste once before.

Both of her parents were Jews from Bethany, but Mattheos, her husband and Timothy's father, was Greek. Their mixed marriage caused so much uproar they had to flee to somewhere safe. They chose Lystra, a small town a few hours' ride north of Tarsus. Most people still spoke their native dialect, not the popular Greek. Protected by a Roman garrison, Lystra was safe. Then she said, "Jerusalem and violence – those words go together. Jerusalem stones the prophets sent to them."

A man rode up alongside them on a horse. "Greetings, friends. Escaping for your lives too?"

Timothy's father answered. "We are returning home. A person can only stand so much celebrating, right?"

"Right. Where is home?"

"Lystra. Came for Passover. Sold a few sheep. Bought some Jerusalem wares. We did not expect such uproar, not on Passover. What about you?"

"My name is Barnabas, from Antioch. I came to celebrate the Passover and to see my cousin. May I go with you, only until I get home? It's best to travel in small groups these days, you know. Not safe to be alone."

"I am Mattheos." Nodding to his wife, he said, "This is Eunice. The boy is Timothy. Your cousin lives in Jerusalem? I feel sorry for him."

"I feel sorry for him too. But probably not for the same reason as you."

"I pity anyone who is a disciple of Jesus…you know, with the Pharisees worked up like they are," Mattheos said.

"It is not what you think. My cousin is one of the Pharisees. He believes that when enough people are converted to Judaism, the Messiah will come. Followers of Jesus are converting good Jewish people to their faith. The Pharisees think these Jesus disciples are delaying the coming of the Messiah and want to stop them," Barnabas explained.

"Interesting. Who is your cousin? Was he at the stoning today?"

"Saul. He was there. He was the one holding the coats. He is serious about cleansing Jerusalem from all the followers of Jesus. That's why I had to leave."

"What do you mean? You are his cousin. You are Jewish. You are safe."

"I may be his cousin. I may be Jewish. But I am not safe. I am a disciple of Jesus. I believe Jesus was the Messiah. Saul would imprison me if he could."

"What are you planning to do?"

"I'm heading home to pray for Saul's transformation. What else can I do? But it is enough."

"You are probably right about prayer. What transformation are you praying for? Why do you think that this Jesus was the Messiah? There have been many to make that claim, right?" asked Mattheos.

"Only Jesus fulfilled hundreds of Jewish prophecies about the Messiah. None of the others even fulfilled two or three of them. He must be the man," said Barnabas. "Right now Saul walks in darkness. I want him to see the light."

"Well, you may be right. Or you may be wrong. I do not

think this is something to die for."

"If you knew in your heart of hearts that Jesus was the Messiah, you would die for him too."

The four rode on in silence. Timothy wondered how anyone could hate Jesus as much as the Pharisees do. He wondered whether Barnabas was correct in whom Jesus really was. As other travelers joined their little band, the conversation turned to discussing whether they would be ambushed by raiding bands of nomads before they reached Damascus.

Timothy took his mother's hand, which was around his waist. "Mother, would you please tell me more about this man named Jesus?"

Eunice smiled and kissed the back of his head. "When we get home, your grandmother will tell us both. She met him once."

Timothy leaned back into his mother's chest and smiled.

 In addition to his illustrious writing career, **Delbert Teachout** has earned a PhD, an MS, and a BA in Psychology. Shalom Ministry, Inc. ordained him into ministry in 2002. He also served in the USAF for 22½ years before retiring as a captain.

Delbert has worked in many lay positions in the church including nursery, children's Sunday school, adult Sunday school, church outreach, and church training. He has also served as Sunday school superintendent and deacon. He further taught Old Testament and New Testament Survey and General Psychology as an adjunct faculty member for Alpena Community College.

Delbert has more than 175 published articles in periodicals, with a combined circulation of over 700,000. He has recently been given the title of Managing Editor for *Halo Magazine*.

Delbert has been married for 38 years and has four children and seven grandchildren.

Bravery Brought Salvation

By Robin Walker

Brenda Ware skipped along as she returned to her house after another blissfully long visit to the park.

Her day had started early. She had been rolled out of bed before 8:00 that morning. She hadn't showered, even though she knew she needed one. No one made her do it, so why bother?

Brenda ate cold rice and uncooked kidney beans for breakfast – typical fare in her home. She would have no lunch, and dinner would be a repeat of breakfast.

She had been told not to come back until late afternoon or early evening. She knew what that meant. *You come back early, and you'll be beaten.*

After her full and uneventful day away, she neared her front stoop. Now that she was so close to the door, caution assumed its familiar position in her mind. She licked her lips, as if the act would somehow help her into the house. Her hands got sweaty, and she rubbed them down her skirt. She forced her breathing down. *Slow. Slower. Come on. You can do it.* Gingerly, quietly, she tiptoed up the steps.

Brenda peered inside the screen and listened. Voices traveled from the dining room. From her vantage point, she could see that two gentlemen sat at the table with her mom.

Gentlemen? Mom never had gentlemen. Men? Yes. But never gentlemen.

As a battle waged inside her tiny chest, Brenda paused before touching the handle. Why were those gentlemen in her house? Why was Mom talking with them? When had they come? Had they interrupted Mom's play? Brenda hoped not. If they had, there was no telling how the night would unfold in the Ware house after dark. Mom didn't seem frustrated. Maybe Brenda was worried over nothing. She seemed tired, though – weary even.

Brenda's mind swirled. She remembered back to a day about eight weeks ago, one with the same morning routine. She had gone to her favorite park that day, too – the familiar growl in her stomach had told her that she must have been there for about four hours. Two boys arrived. She had never seen them before, but she didn't worry. Not too much. She could tell they were bigger than her, but they were dressed nice – usually the mean boys were the ones with holes in the knees of their jeans and dirty knit caps wedged on their heads. If these boys had looked like that, Brenda would have gotten out of there as fast as her legs could carry her.

The two had played by themselves for a short time and then came over to the swings, where Brenda sat perched on her favorite weathered piece of rounded rubber in the whole world.

"Give us your swing," they had said. Brenda ignored them. There were at least three or four others available. They didn't need hers.

The boys had repeated their demand twice more and then took action. One on each side of her, they had each grabbed a swing. Before Brenda could think or even react, the swings had found their mark.

The first hit had stunned her to the point of making her immobile. During the onslaught that followed, she had finally found her wits. She stopped her swing and fell to the ground. She half-crawled out of the area to put some distance between her and her tormentors.

The boys had taken their prizes. They swung for a short time, taking only four or five pumps, before jumping off. Then, running off the playground, they laughed as they made their way down the block.

As Brenda stumbled home, she had become fearful. She knew it was too early to arrive back at the house. What would she do when she got there? Her mind whirled between the reality of the situation and her extreme pain. She clenched her jaw, determined to keep from crying. *Look at all of these cars and trucks passing me,* she had thought. *Can't they see me? Can't they see that I need help? I can barely walk! Don't they care about me at all? Does anyone?*

Where is that kind lady from this morning, the one with the gum?

Brenda had left the house that morning with her own treasured piece of gum. She had saved it from a half-used packet that she had found in the gutter a few days before. Sure, the sticks had been a little damp, but that wasn't anything a night on a quiet window sill wouldn't cure. She had looked around to make sure no one was watching before popping the stick into her mouth. *Oh, cinnamon!* Her favorite.

Chewing all the sweetness out of her treasure as she walked, Brenda must have smiled in anticipation of what the day might bring. And at the height of her anticipation, the gum had fallen out of her mouth and into the dirt. Brenda watched, helplessly, as a community of tiny, black ants laid claim to it. All she could do was stand there and cry, feeling ever so sorry for herself. That lady had come out of nowhere and had presented her with a fresh, wrapped stick. Brenda had wondered at the time if that lady was an angel. She was nowhere in sight now.

Brenda knew the rules and the times. When Mom played, no

one could come into the house. Mom was at play when Brenda finally found her front porch.

How had she gotten there? She hadn't a clue.

She had waited on the front porch for what seemed like forever. Finally the pain became so unbearable that she felt like she had to go inside for help.

All Brenda remembered after that was the constant pounding, all over her already sore body. She had retreated back outside to the porch as soon as she could get away again.

Brenda had no idea how long it had been before Mom came out of the house. She was mad, completely upset at Brenda. She had said that her men folks were leaving early and that it was all Brenda's fault again.

It was never Mom's fault.

Brenda had been confused at the time. It confused her still. *How could Mom not see that I was bruised and bleeding already? How could she heap more pain onto me?* She had tried to explain why she had come home early. Mom had ignored her, staring after the cars as they pulled onto the street.

When she had nothing else to occupy her time or attention, Mom had asked Brenda why she hadn't just given up her swing. Mom said that Brenda wouldn't have had to come home and bring all this trouble with her. She had reached out to slap Brenda – once, twice, then in a storm of hits, pushes and jabs. She had chanted, "It's all your fault," with every slap.

In Brenda's battered state, she had begun to silently agree with her mother. *How could a child do so much wrong in one day and hurt her mom so much?* Brenda just couldn't have let her mom have any fun or any time to herself, could she?

Mom had screamed at Brenda for causing all the day's troubles. She said that Brenda had been so stingy with those swings – swings that weren't even hers.

"No way are we going to the hospital or to the doctors,"

Mom had screamed. "I'm tired of people blaming me for everything you kids do wrong. Can't they see that my kids are just really bad?" Swat. Swat. Swat. They would walk to Peg's house instead and have her treat the wounds.

Peg, a nurse and a close family friend, had wanted to take them to get medical treatment. "Treat her here yourself, or she'll get no treatment," Mom had said. Her face looked flat, as flat as her words sounded.

Peg had done her best. By the time they left, Brenda had made mental notes on how to change her wraps. She knew she would have to do it all by herself if it was going to get done.

Brenda sighed now, thinking back on it all. She had done well with the care of her wounds. She had no scabs. No scars. All better, at least on the outside. She still had to leave the house most every morning, but at least the weather was nice. The park was pleasant, as long as those boys didn't show up again.

Now here she was at her front door again, squinting into the screen in hopes of discovering what she could expect on the other side, before she had to face it head on. Something was eating at her. She had a need she couldn't name, and it urged her toward the dining room. It was like she didn't have a choice.

Was she crazy?

No, not this time. This time, Brenda simply felt at peace with her decision. She went straight to the dining room table, where the three still sat. Brenda listened as Mom said that she wasn't interested in Jesus. When the gentlemen asked if they could pray before leaving, Mom rolled her eyes and looked away. "Yes. I guess that'd be all right." She folded her arms in tight against her belly, as if she braced for a blow.

The gentlemen prayed about their thankfulness. They prayed about salvation that was free to all who were willing to accept it. In the end, they said, "Amen," and stood to leave. Reacting, not thinking, Brenda reached out and grabbed a suit coat sleeve. The man looked down at her and smiled.

"Is Jesus for kids?"

"Most definitely," both men said in harmony.

Without even asking Mrs. Ware's permission, Brenda accepted the free and perfect plan of salvation that these gentlemen laid out before her. She didn't know what to expect after they left, but it didn't matter. Not now.

At the young age of eight, Brenda had someone she could call her own, someone that no one and nothing could take away from her or destroy. Someone she could always trust and who would and always did love her. A father, brother, savior, and guide, this Jesus loved her just because she was Brenda. Even at her age, or maybe *because of* it, she knew that promise would never be broken. She held it tightly. It would hold her against every cutting remark in time to come. It would shield her against the abuse and mistreatment. It would cover her like a blanket when the cold of the night cut her through to the bone. Thanks be to God for His unflappable, unending, amazing love.

The Biography for our contributor, Robin Walker is, unfortunately, unavailable.

From Suicide to Ministry

By Dennis Snyder

Jim's eyes bulged, and his heart threatened to burst out of his chest. He had called home at 3:25, five minutes before clock out. He did it every day. She hadn't answered. *She always answers.*

He dialed again, tapping his steel-toed boot as the rotary phone took its slow, deliberate time. Nothing but a busy signal.

Leaving the pay phone's receiver to dangle and clang against the cinderblock wall, he bolted to his locker. Leather jacket. Sunglasses. Keys. Storming toward the exit, he tied a dew rag onto his head before freeing his ponytail from beneath the jacket collar. He breezed through the door and into the sun.

Ever at the ready, his motorcycle glinted at him from the parking lot, challenging him to go full throttle. He ran toward it, knowing he would take that challenge. One kick-start and it roared to life, transporting him home at breakneck speed.

* * * * *

Draped over the bed, one arm dangling off the side just fingertips from an empty pill bottle laid a motionless body. Prone, her face was buried in the pillow. The beep, beep, beep of the phone wailed in the background.

"No!" Jim rolled his wife over. "Sally, what have you done? Why?"

He cursed. *Who'd you expect to answer that stupid question?*

He grabbed the bottle and phone. Depressing the receiver to clear the line, he read the words Valium on the paper glued to the bottle. He released the receiver and dialed the emergency number Sally had taped to the phone's cradle.

Waiting for what seemed like hours, he checked her for a pulse. He allowed a deep, cleansing exhale when he felt a faint heartbeat.

"Come on...hurry up...get here...!" He stretched the words out under his breath, trying to slow his racing heart. It didn't work. "I'm not ready to give up on the love of my life." Feeling moisture on his cheeks, he cradled Sally's head and stroked her long blond hair.

"Lord, don't let her die," he whispered. The words jolted him out of his angst, if only for a moment. When was the last time he had thought to pray?

* * * * *

"Hmm," Sally groaned, gingerly rocking her head, in an attempt to clear it from the fog she surely found herself in.

Jim ached for her. Ached for himself.

She raised her hand to her eyes and tried to sit up. "What happened? Where am I?"

"Just sit back. You're in the hospital." He shook his head, both frustrated and hurt. "Don't you remember what you did?"

She looked to the side and found blinking lights on a monitor. Her hand slid down the wires attached to her chest. The other hand explored the oxygen tube irritating her nostrils. "Oh, Lord. Yes. Yes. I remember. It was horrible." She closed her eyes and began to cry. "Donna said we could adopt the baby."

"Yeah, I know." Jim leaned in, trying to read her face. "We agreed that it was a good thing, didn't we? You were happy about that."

"You know I was!"

"Then why did you—"

"She came in and threw some candy bars on the break room table—"

"Sally—"

"For a celebration—"

"You're not making sense."

She sat up and looked at him. Tears streamed down her cheeks, but he had no doubt that she was fully awake. Fully coherent.

"When I asked what we were celebrating, Donna said she'd just had an abortion."

The words blew him back with hurricane force. "What?"

"She killed our baby, Jim! She killed—"

"Sweetie," Jim's voice was lost as he struggled with his own tears. He rose, his arms encircling her, cords and all. He squeezed her ever so gently, hoping he didn't hurt anything. He managed to croak, "I'm so sorry. So sorry."

The words hung just over her head. He felt so helpless. She needed him now, needed to hear…something…something not moronic from him. But he couldn't think of a worthwhile or encouraging thing to say.

He reluctantly released her, sensing her fatigue, knowing she needed to lie back again. He settled himself back on the chair beside her. She melted into the sheets. But his eyes never left hers.

His hand found hers. Minutes ticked by as they stared into one another's tear stained faces. Each seemed oblivious to the gray-haired nurse tending to the monitor and the intravenous needle. The nurse spoke as she fluffed the bed pillow, rousing them both.

"Well, young lady, you swallowed enough pills to kill an elephant." Leaning closer to Sally, she whispered, "Somebody up there must really like you."

Sally looked up at her, her eyes met with a wrinkled smile.

Nodding toward Jim, the nurse said, "Your man hasn't left your side since they brought you in. He's a keeper."

"Thank you." Sally shed tears anew, turning her head toward Jim. "He's the reason I'm still here."

Jim sat up and leaned in again. "Did I miss something in that conversation?"

Sally took both of his hands. "Right before I passed out, I realized I had made a huge mistake." She sobbed and groaned, but her words wouldn't be denied. "I was so selfish. I never gave you a thought. All I could think about was that baby. The baby I would never hold. I—"

"I'm just so glad you're okay and—"

"Shh. Please. I have to say this."

Jim sat back, as if to give her the full room. "I'm sorry, baby. Go ahead."

She nodded. She cleared her throat. "All of a sudden, I thought about you and what taking my life would do. I knew you would've blamed yourself. I tried to reach for the phone but knocked it to the floor. So, I called out to God. I told Him that if He let me live I would do whatever I could to learn more about Him."

He shifted uncomfortably. His eyes dropped to his hands. He just couldn't look into those eyes right now, not with the confusion he was feeling. "Why would you think He could help?"

"I don't know. I just felt it was the thing to do. All I knew was that I no longer wanted to die. I love you too much to put you through that."

The nurse interrupted once again, this time with instructions. "Mr. Tiller, you're gonna have to leave for a while. Your wife needs to get some rest. The cafeteria's open, and they serve a pretty good lunch. Why don't you go down and eat?"

"I am awfully tired, honey," Sally said. "You've been here all night. Why don't you do what the nurse says? Go on home. Take a shower and a nap. I'll be okay."

The nurse jumped in. "That's a great idea. Don't worry, Mr. Tiller. We'll take good care of her. I promise."

Jim hesitated for a moment. "Okay. But I'll be back in two hours. I need to call the boss and tell him I won't be in for a few days." He nodded toward Sally. "I guess I should call work for you, too."

Sighing, she said, "Okay, but just tell them I'm sick – not that I did this stupid thing."

"This will be just between you and me, baby." Jim leaned down to give her a kiss on the forehead.

* * * * *

Sally woke to the sound of dishes clanking in the kitchen. The smell of bacon wafted through the house, making her smile. *Maybe it was all a dream.*

Her face fell as she noticed the fall flower arrangement all but overtaking her nightstand. Not that she didn't like flowers. She loved them. But as good a guy as Jim was, he didn't typically buy flowers. And he never made breakfast.

Did Donna really abort the baby?

Was I foolish enough to try to kill myself?

Swinging her legs over the side of the bed, she felt the emptiness in her stomach along with a few twinges of pain. Her mind cleared, and she knew the truth.

"Hey, you're already up," Jim said as he breezed into the room. "I was just coming to wake you for breakfast. How ya feeling this morning?"

"Tell me it never happened."

"Come on, Babe." Jim felt helpless all over again. "It's all right. We'll get through this together."

"I am so sorry," Sally said. She tried to hold the tears back, but she just couldn't. "I've made such a mess of things. It was nothing you did. You're the best thing that has ever happened to me. I love you, you know. I love you with all my heart. I would never want to hurt you."

Jim dropped to the bed and gathered Sally in his arms. "I know. I love you, too."

When the quakes in her body subsided and her breathing regained its normal rhythm, Jim said, "You'll feel better when you've had something to eat, don't you think?" He shook her a little, hoping to cheer her up. "Come on. You don't get to sample my eggs every day...well, actually, I guess you've never sampled them." It was enough to get a little giggle out of her. He smiled, too. "Let's eat while everything's still hot."

Sally seemed so fragile, so weak. She leaned on Jim as he helped her up. He carried her more than he led her to the kitchen table.

"Wow. Look at this." Sally seemed excited as she swept her hand over the table setting, but her mood quickly changed. "I don't deserve all of this."

He wouldn't let her go to that dark place in her mind again, not so soon. He gripped her a little tighter and eased her into her chair before kissing her at her temple. "Hope you like it," he said. "I worked hard on it."

Sitting across from one another, they ate without a word. Jim ate, at least. He looked at her between bites and saw that she just stared at her food, moving it around with her fork. "Okay, you're not eating. It's not that bad, is it?"

"Of course not." Sally smiled.

"What's going through that pretty little head of yours?" he

asked with a cock of his head.

She put her fork down and looked intently into her husband's eyes, "Honey, we need to find a church to go to. I promised God that, if He let me live, I would find out more about Him. The only place I know of is in church."

"We're not going to fit into any church that I know of. Look at me – can you imagine a guy like me there? I'd never fit in. Every churchgoer I know looks like they just stepped out of Ozzie and Harriet. That's not us, Honey."

"I know, but I've gotta find out why He kept me alive. You heard the nurse. I should have died."

"Okay." Jim sighed and pushed his plate away. "I'll take you to church. But don't expect them to accept us."

"We'll try the one at the end of the road this Sunday. Find out what time they start. I don't want to get there early." He gave her a half smile.

He stood, stretching. "You gonna be all right if I head into work for a couple of hours? They're getting behind and need me to set some things up."

"Yeah, go ahead. I'll be fine. I need to call my mom. She's gonna wonder why I haven't called in a few days."

* * * * *

The next Sunday, Jim and Sally walked into the church on the end of the road. Immediately, Jim remembered the only Bible story he had ever heard – it was just like the parting of the Red Sea as church people cleared a path for the two of them. Not one handshake or greeting – simply a bulletin placed in their hands by some old guy standing at the door.

The service over and the pair safely sitting in their own car, Jim said, "I don't know about you, Sally, but if that's what God is about, no, thank you."

"I'll agree with you, Honey. I don't think we'll find out anything about God there. My mom said she met some people at her church last week. They just got transferred to Maryland. Maybe they had a church here in South Shore that we could visit?"

"I don't know. Your mom's church is awfully religious for me. But then, any church has to be better than this one. See if you can find out by next Sunday. I'd like to get this church thing over with as soon as we can."

* * * * *

Plopping down in the easy chair, dirty sweat rolling down his face, Jim took a long drink of ice water. Rolling the cold, wet glass across his forehead, he said, "We have enough wood to last us through the winter. I'm glad it is all done. I think I'll go fishing in the morning."

"Oh, honey, we have church in the morning."

Jim's jaw dropped. "What? You didn't mention anything about church. I figured you never heard from your mom.

"You're right. I didn't hear from her, but I got a call from the pastor of the Baptist church east of town. The lady Mom met called him and gave him our number. He invited us to come to their church tomorrow. I said we would be there."

"Man, those Baptists are all Jesus freaks. I don't want anything to do with them. I'm not going."

"The head honcho himself called and invited us. I said we would go. Come on, Jim. Please."

"Okay, but just this once. If you want to go back, make some friends. One time is too many for me. Those guys are way too religious."

Sunday morning, Jim and Sally walked into the Eastside Baptist Church smelling of leather and stale cigarette smoke. Less than two feet into the door, a young man shook Jim's hand and introduced himself. Within minutes, he was surrounded by others welcoming him into their midst. Sally found herself talking with ladies, young and old, as she tried to stay close to Jim. They were ushered into the sanctuary, given bulletins, and seated.

"Wow, what a difference," Jim said, leaning close to his wife. "They actually seemed interested in us."

Sally nodded as everyone stood to begin singing.

When the pastor began his message, he said, "If you folks would all take out your Bibles and turn to Ephesians 2:8-10, we'll get this preaching on the road."

On the drive home, Sally asked, "Well, what did you think?"

"I don't know what to think," said Jim as he shook his head. "They have something I've never seen before. And did you see? The pastor actually preached from the Bible. It wasn't just his opinion on things. He actually read from it. I think I want to go back again next week."

"What? Aren't you the one who said they were nothing but Jesus freaks?"

"That was before I met them." Jim smiled. "They actually wanted to know more about us. They seemed to genuinely care. I've gotta learn more about this Jesus Christ the pastor talked about. You do want to go back, don't you?"

"Yeah, I guess if you do, I do," she said, somewhat in shock. "It was different. I didn't think you would want to go back."

The rest of the story:

Jim and Sally continued attending church Sunday morning and evening and trusted Christ as their Lord and Savior three months later. They eventually went back to Bible College. Jim has been serving as a senior pastor, with his wife faithfully ministering at his side, for over 27 years.

Eight years after their conversion to Christ, four weeks after graduating from college, Jim and Sally adopted their son. Three days before they were to finalize the adoption process, they were told that Sally was six weeks pregnant. They have a son (married) and daughter (married). Their beautiful granddaughter is the apple of their eyes. God is good all the time.

 **Dennis Snyder** is the pastor of a local church in Michigan. He and his wife of 42 years are the proud parents of two adult children and the grandparents of a beautiful granddaughter. When Dennis is not writing or preaching, he enjoys spending time with his wife, riding his Harley, and golfing.

Dennis is the author of the *Looking at Life Through the Grid of the Bible*, a self-directed Bible study series. He is also the author of the *Lake Haven Murders* mystery series and the novel *Yellow Rose of Texas*. Dennis is also the CEO and publisher of Concerning Life Publishing located in Spring Lake, Michigan.

Patsy the Runaway

By Maria De Lugt Kocsis

Patsy stiffened when she heard the key in the lock. She had been dreaming that she was back at home in her own bed.

"Get up," Clark said harshly. "Time to perform."

She lifted her weary body out of bed. She stood up, not bothering to cover her body.

The skimpy nightgown that now hung loosely was way too big for her. "Not bad," said a second male voice. She blocked out the rest of the conversation. Going through the motions, she let her body be used until the man was satisfied. "Oh, God, help me," she silently prayed.

* * * * *

I remember the first time I saw Patsy. She looked at me with those big, blue, expressive eyes – eyes that held a puzzled, questioning, wondering look. What was going on now? She was only four years old and could not understand why her mommy was not here with her brothers and her daddy at Christmas.

It was the evening of Christmas Day. I had spoken to her dad Rick the day before and found out that his wife had left him and the four kids. "Come on over to my house tomorrow," I told him. "There will be plenty of food left over from Christmas Eve."

So he and the four kids came with sad looks on their faces. I had a little present for each of them, and we enjoyed a little piece of Christmas joy together.

Twelve years later, Rick and I sat in a booth across from each other at a local coffee shop. He told me how Patsy had dropped out of school, run away, and then called home several weeks after Rick had reported her missing. They had posted her picture all over town on milk cartons, bulletin boards, and telephone poles but to no avail. She finally called home after seeing her face on a milk carton. Not that it helped any. She had refused to come home. She said she was happy. Rick did not believe her. Unfortunately, according to the police, she was sixteen and there was not a thing he could do to bring her home.

* * * * *

At first, Patsy was a little frightened but excited. A handsome man named Clark had promised her that she could do and have whatever she wanted if she came with him. She didn't have to put up with rules anymore. She didn't have to go to school, have curfews, or do chores. And he had promised her more of the pills that he had given to her to make her pain go away and make her feel good. She didn't have to think about whether to accept his offer. He told her to pack her suitcase and meet him at the corner the next morning at 9:00, after everyone else left the house.

The night before, Patsy had quietly taken her suitcase off the basement shelf, accidentally knocking over a box with Christmas ornaments. Thankfully, no one heard her. She quietly walked up to her room and put her suitcase under her bed. After everyone had gone to bed, she packed what clothes she could. She couldn't wait to leave and meet Clark so that she could begin to do whatever she wanted. What exactly that was, she didn't know. But she was sure she would be happier. She hardly slept that night.

The next morning, Patsy was up early, happy and excited. Her dad asked her what her day would be like, and she said, "Oh, nothing special. Just the usual."

At 9:00, she was waiting at the corner, just as she had been instructed. Clark drove up in a big limousine, and she got in. "Where are we going?" Patsy asked.

"You'll see," Clark said, with a smirk.

They drove for hours, stopping just to use the restrooms. She saw the signs showing the state names: Ohio, Kentucky, Tennessee, Georgia, and finally Florida. They stopped in front of a night club called The Strip Joint.

"What is that?" Patsy asked.

"Come on in and see for yourself." Clark took Patsy by the arm and introduced her to the owner.

"Isn't she a little young?"

"Oh, no. With some makeup, she'll do just fine."

The owner looked Patsy up and down. He opened up her jacket to see her tank top. "Yeah, she'll do," he said.

Patsy and Clark left. Clark took her to an apartment that consisted of one large room with a bed and a sofa. The sofa was a pull-out bed. "That's where you'll sleep," Clark said, nodding toward it.

Clark handed her a skimpy, two-piece swimsuit. "Here. Try this on. Let me see you in it."

Patsy looked at him with big eyes. "I don't wear anything this skimpy," she said.

"You will now. Don't worry. You'll wear something over it part of the time. Then you can take that off, too. Here. You can wear this under the bottom of the suit." He handed her something that looked like just a couple of strings.

"But that covers nothing!" she said.

"That's the general idea," Clark said. "Here are some pills. This will help you get over your self-consciousness." Gratefully, Patsy swallowed them dry.

"I'll pick you up around 8:00 a.m. There's some food in the fridge." Clark pointed to a small refrigerator under the counter, in the corner. He turned on his heel and walked out of the apartment, leaving Patsy by herself.

Exhausted, Patsy dropped to the sofa and promptly fell asleep.

Patsy awakened with a start. She felt as though she had just closed her eyes, but someone was opening the apartment door. She jumped up and saw Clark standing on the threshold. "Time to get ready," he said. "I brought you some makeup. Be sure to put a lot on." She just stood there, unable to move. "Well, hurry up," he said.

Patsy stumbled to the bathroom. With trembling hands, she started to change into the swimsuit Clark had presented to her earlier. *What have I gotten myself into?*

Time was a blur. Before Patsy knew it, she and Clark were walking back into the strip club. Whistles, cat calls, and applause greeted her. The pills were working. All this attention she was getting – *I must look really good!*

Not knowing what to do, Patsy hung back. Not for long. The owner approached her. "Come on, girlie. If you want to work, you'll have to perform."

The room was packed with men of all ages and all sizes, along with all kinds of sweat, smell, and odor. One or two men leered at her, pinching her bottom and grabbing her top as she walked by. She hesitated. Someone gave her a shove. She fell on her knees.

"Cut that out!" Clark said from somewhere in the crowd. "This one's new at the game."

She watched what the other girls did, attempting to follow

their moves. Slowly she became accustomed to her surroundings, to what Clark expected of her.

This schedule, this lifestyle, went on night after night. Weeks turned to months and months to years.

Patsy was furnished with a steady supply of pills and any food she wanted. But she was not let out of Clark's sight, other than when she was left alone in her apartment. He always locked the door behind him when he left, and Patsy had no way out.

Clark would come and get her or would stay with her until it was time to leave, time to go back to work.

After a time, Clark began threatening her. He said, "If you try to run, I'll come after you!"

Can he read me that well? Patsy thought. *Does it show that much?*

Other times Clark would threaten to cut off her supply of drugs. "If you're not a good girl, I'll cut off your pills."

He watched Patsy every minute that she was out of the apartment. She had no telephone and was forbidden contact with anyone other than Clark. When she wasn't working, Clark kept her in a near comatose state within the walls of the apartment.

It was the second year anniversary of Patsy's flight to freedom. *Some freedom,* she thought. *How could I have been such a fool?* She missed her family, her friends, and her school. She missed the birthdays, the Christmases, and all the other holidays that her family had celebrated together – all those times she had taken for granted before running away with Clark.

Patsy wondered how her brothers were doing. She started having dreams about them, imaging how they were growing and thriving without her there to see it. *What have I done to myself? Is it too late for me?*

Patsy awakened one morning from a stupor. Nothing new. Before long, Clark would come to give her the morning pills she had come to expect. Then she would go to work and perform until she nearly dropped. Then Clark would bring her back to the apartment and give her more pills to settle her down. Settle her down – more like put her completely under. Today, though, she had a new thought. Today would be different.

Several weeks before, her father had tracked her down through some detectives he had hired. He had begged her to come home. He said he had contacted the police but that they couldn't do anything since she was over sixteen.

Patsy had tried to tell her father that she was happy so that he wouldn't worry. When he wouldn't back down, she had come a little closer to the truth. She told him that it was too late for her. She said that all the horrible things she had done and the pain she had caused – she didn't deserve to come home.

"No, no, no! You are forgiven! Please, please come home!"

Her conscience, numbed and ignored for so long, began to come alive again.

When Clark showed up with Patsy's morning dosage, she pretended to take them. Then she tried to act like she always did, so as not to arouse any suspicions.

* * * * *

When Rick and I met for coffee, he told me all he knew of Patsy's story. On an impulse, I grabbed his hand and prayed. "Lord, if it is your will, please speak to this girl's heart and help her to come home."

The next morning, Rick called me with great excitement. He told me Patsy had telephoned him to say that she had prayed and asked God to help her. She said that He had made a way for her to escape. She was on her way home!

"Your God must be a very powerful God to have heard your prayers," Rick said.

Patsy came home and let God transform her. She said

goodbye to the life that she thought would bring freedom but brought only pain and chains instead. She finished high school and went on to college. She now has a nursing career and is a happy young woman.

We serve a God of second chances. Patsy is living proof.

 **Maria De Lugt Kocsis** was a realtor for 32 years, and before that she spent 19 years in Corporate America. A Dutch Naturalized Citizen, she was born in The Hague, The Netherlands.

She is proud of her Dutch heritage, although she considers herself an American Patriot. She emigrated in 1950 with her parents and seven of her 10 siblings. Maria has had many interesting experiences throughout her life and is putting those stories in writing. She discovered late in life her love of writing and photography, among other interests.

God shed His grace on Maria throughout her life. She lives in Grand Rapids and has two wonderful children and three grandchildren who are the light of her life. You may contact Maria at MariaKocsis@grar.com. This memoir is one of two she has written for *The Transformation Project*.

The Beautiful Sorrow

By Diana Geisel

Among the paradoxes of life gently lies the beautiful sorrow. The sorrow that you feel after someone you have loved has departed this world, yet you hold that great assurance that they are now home safe and sheltered in the arms of God. When our beloved daughter, Shari, left her mortal, medically fragile, 39-year-old body behind, she put on immortality. My first response as her mother and the closest person on earth to her was an incredible feeling that she was finally safe. Safe from society and government interference, safe from illness and injury and from the unknown medical conditions she harbored in her body, and safe from the work of death. She was safe from the labor that characterizes the departure from earth to entrance into the Kingdom of Heaven.

She had no doubts about Heaven. Nor do I have any doubts about Heaven. Others may mock or doubt, but to quote the words of an old hymn, "I have a hope that will surely endure after the passing of time." This hope that God has placed deeply within my soul gives me that peace that passes all understanding. In spite of the fact that in the last seven months I have lost my daughter-in -law to brain cancer, my daughter to septic infection, and my brother-in-law to diabetes, I do not sorrow as those who have no hope. I do not get enraged or angry with God or anyone else. I simply know that God is harvesting a great number of those I love to His side and that they are all safe. That is a beautiful reality.

I have been told by experts in the field that it is unusual for a severely physically impaired person not to be severely mentally impaired also. It is even rarer for a person who also has cognitive disabilities to understand spiritual things. Shari was one of those rare people. She understood human nature and the things of God, yet she did not understand money or time. We always told her that she was smart and beautiful, and she believed it to be so. She showed great compassion and concern for others. When her sister-in-law Diane and respite caretaker of 20 years was diagnosed with brain cancer and given a limited survival time, Shari sat by her bedside day after day. Although it was hard for her to reach Diane, she got as close to her bed as her wheelchair would allow. She reached out for her hand and gently caressed the back of Diane's hand with her thumb. It was a tender picture of the patient bringing comfort to the caretaker. Shari did not miss any opportunity to sit by Diane's bedside. She grieved as deeply as the rest of us when Diane took her last breath.

In the account found in John 11:21-27, Mary and Martha were grieving the loss of their dear brother Lazarus. Jesus especially loved Martha, Mary, and Lazarus. By the time Jesus arrived, Lazarus had been in the grave four days. Martha heard Jesus was coming and went out to meet Him. On the basis of this passage, Shari's father John sat down with her and asked three questions.

First he asked, "Shari, why do (we) or good people suffer?"

She thought for a moment and then gave several answers to this. "Suffering doesn't have anything to do with whether they're good or bad. Because that's in God's plan for some reason, but not to worry, because after you're done suffering, God will take you and your suffering will be over with soon enough." Then she gave the most honest of answers one can give. "I don't know."

Secondly, John asked Shari, "How can we trust in hope? How do we find hope?"

Shari's simple answer could have made a sermon taken from Matthew 6:32. She reasoned, "_Ask_ God for what you need and pray and _trust_ God _knows_ what you need. If He thinks you need it you'll have it."

When Shari understood that now her time on earth would soon be over, too, she did not cry or express fear. She embraced death as she had embraced her limitations in life. The third question gives us insight into how she could die so peacefully without tears or struggle. John asked, "Shari, what brings _you_ hope?" I will never forget her answer. It was as if it had been lifted right from the passage in John 11:25-26. "Knowing that when I die I'll go to heaven, which means that I'll never die."

It is wonderment to me that God can take something ugly or deformed under earthly circumstances and cause you to see it as beautiful. I experienced one such moment when my husband had open-heart surgery. Afterward, he felt badly about having a large scar running down the full length of his chest. As he examined the scar in the mirror, I gently touched his scar, running my finger down the length of it. "Please don't feel badly. That scar is beautiful to me. I love that scar. That scar gave us more time together. I will always look tenderly at that scar." In a similar special moment, when Shari lay in her bed, dying, her deformed and fragile legs and skin, with her swollen club feet were exposed from under the sheet. She always wanted to wear shoes. However, she never could because, in her own words, her feet were shaped like footballs. In that moment I pondered how beautiful those ugly legs and feet were to me. When someone is precious to you, something unsightly has a way of taking on a beauty that is truly only in the eye and heart of the beholder, who is looking through the eyes of love.

She was so grateful for everything we did for her. She had such limited use of her arms and no use of her legs. Literally just about everything had to be done for her, but she was so patient with those doing it. She expressed a "Thank you" for each task you did for her. One day when she was deathly ill, she raised her head and weakly said to me, "Mom, thank you for not sending me to a parentless home." Her driving passion was for her and her family to be together. She treasured her time with us and looked forward to our many family holidays together.

Today, when I remember Shari, I do not recall how hard her care was or how limited she was or how confined we were. I don't recall how difficult it was to provide clothes for her twisted body or how hard it was to transport her or move her. I don't recall how her grip on reality was slipping or how poor her memory was becoming. I don't focus on her life of pain, surgery, and brokenness. I recall her beautiful spirit, her wit, her love. Not a day passed without her saying at least once, "Mom, have I told you yet today that I love you?" No one will ever love me like that again.

Being at peace about the timing of her departure and the destination of her trip or recalling the beauty of her life does not exempt any of us from the work of grief. Some nights we go to bed with a deep heartache and wake in the morning with it still gripping our hearts. We still walk about in disbelief that she was here and is now mysteriously gone. Even so, when I look back, I am both content with her home-going and deeply saddened by her absence. It is one of life's many paradoxes. It is a beautiful sorrow.

Even as a child **Diana Geisel** enjoyed writing, and she looked forward to those classes that gave her the opportunity to write creatively.

Recently she wrote for a large audience of family and friends when her daughter and daughter-in-law became ill. Both died within months of each other. She received such encouragement about the spiritual tone of that writing that she began to ask the Lord if writing was within His plan for her. She is still exploring that question, asking God if there is a writer inside. If so, she is asking Him to bring that gift to the surface, increase her skills, and let that flow for His glory and His kingdom.

Diana is currently writing memoirs but would like to move into the inspirational fiction genre, both for adults and children; she sees a big need for character building fiction for children in particular. Visit her blog at http://djgeisel.wordpress.com. This memoir is one of four she has written for *The Transformation Project.*

Becoming Family

Nancy Bouwens

We stood before a smattering of friends and family full of hope. A crisp Thursday evening in September was the backdrop as we promised love, commitment, and faithfulness forever. We had chosen a weeknight for our wedding because it worked for us. Weddings are not usually held in the middle of the week, but we had a mere 72 hours before we were expected back at work on Monday morning. Those we loved the most gathered on a dusky evening in the small Midwestern Lutheran church where I had grown up. Husband to be and I stood close, holding hands and fighting back tears of joy as we celebrated the moment that was now and the anticipation of a future yet to come.

Vows were spoken and hugs exchanged with our guests. We invited them to join us for the first of many meals we planned to share as husband and wife. It was a simple array of food brought by generous friends and family—their contribution to our wedding celebration. My parents had come with a large bright yellow glass bowl filled with sweet cherry tomatoes grown from the dark earth of their garden. Thick yeasty rolls from a local bakery were served alongside steaming bowls of homemade potato soup made by our own hands that morning.

Love, laughter, and the opening of wedding gifts were followed by slices of banana nut cake topped with creamy sweetness. We finished our cake and ran to the car amidst shouts of "good luck" and "congratulations" as clear autumn evening skies began to threaten rain.

Our hearts were full and happy. We had each other, love, and the promise of a life together. We were two separate people becoming one and choosing to leave all others behind. It was not possible on our wedding Thursday, filled with promise, to see what was ahead for Husband and me.

This was as it should be. Our hearts were full.

Newly wedded couples – whether on dusky fall evenings, hot summer Saturdays, or Fridays in the spring – are most often unaware of the hard places of life to come. We too were blind.

We soon were faced with the reality of what perhaps we knew all along. Making vows, building a house, speaking promises, sharing toothpaste, buying groceries, and even birthing Baby Girl does not create a family.

Evening walks, chocolate chip cookies, and the sound of sprinklers hitting a fresh cut lawn on muggy summer evenings wove together with the stiffness of sharp words, misunderstandings, too many bills at the end of a month and baggage from our past. All challenged the fragile hope and the foundation of the life we shared.

Both of us had come to the other carrying parcels of brokenness. Prior relationships had shattered our dreams and brought each of us great pain. We had been introduced to each other through mutual friends and family several years earlier, but we had not personally known each other until a few short months before our wedding Thursday. We both were raw and jagged from abuse and abandonment in our past lives. We could not know how the weight of yesterday's baggage would clutter and confuse our future as we stood holding hands on our wedding day.

We had both experienced the pain of broken promises in our past relationships and were determined our marriage would not meet the same fate. Current statistics show 67% of second marriages break apart. Odds are even higher when, like ours, remarriage occurs less than a year after a divorce. Our freight train of hurt was traveling on a wrong way track at a high rate of speed. The possibility of a failed marriage loomed large within our home.

A sticky summer evening, which should have been spent drinking lemonade or pushing a stroller with Baby Girl, became another tangle of sharp words. The harshness of accusations spoken became arrows slicing to the core of our being. We volleyed pain back and forth, but as the moments began to freeze in time and words were cast into the night, I could no longer recall how it had started.

It was surreal. I felt as though I was on the outside of a terrible dream from which I could not wake up. This could not be my life. This could not be our family. We were like two wounded animals flailing in our pain. The train was headed for imminent disaster. Our words were ugly, hard, and hurtful. And on this night, all things became different.

I followed my husband of less than a year from the living room to our newly decorated bedroom. He began to pull random items from closet shelves and toss them into an open suitcase last used for honeymoon joy as he prepared to walk away from his bride and baby daughter.

I knew it was not only his fault; it was mine too. I could not place blame on his choice to leave, for I too had thought of doing the same. Words spilled from my lips in desperation as time rushed by and then stood still in an instant. Deep within I knew life would never be the same if he walked out the door of our little ranch bungalow.

In desperation, I began to grab clothes from his suitcase with the same randomness which he had tossed them in moments before. I threw them across the bedroom, toward the closet where they came from. I could feel hot, painful tears of loss streaming from my eyes.

Babe in arms, standing in the doorway, I pleaded with him to stop as he tried to quickly step beyond my broken heart, his head down, not meeting my eyes and not wanting to even brush against me. We moved like ragged boxers, at the end of a fight, bobbing to and fro in the doorway…trying to win the battle, both exhausted in body and spirit.

Hurting people hurt others. If I didn't know it before, I knew it now. We were both guilty. And now we had turned it onto each other.

The moment played in slow motion as if on an old movie projector screen. I stepped aside, sensing the weight of what was happening as I moved from the doorway. He was leaving, and our family would be no more. Love, resolve, and good intentions had not been enough.

He stood still. I did the same. Baby Girl was silent. The movie reel of broken promises spun out of control as our eyes finally inched toward one another. Tears brimmed and spilled from his and mine as the dance of ragged boxers came to a halt. Not knowing who reached first and realizing it no longer mattered who was right or wrong, we began to cling to each other so tightly that breath was barely possible. Baby Girl's head with her hair barely there collected our tears as our bodies were wracked with sobs amidst the reality of what had almost happened.

Huge tears flowed with abandon as we swayed together in the setting-sun-drenched doorway, hanging onto life and love and God. I could hear the distant drone of neighborhood conversations continuing over backyard fences just beyond where we held each other. No one outside our walls could have known a family had almost splintered just a few short yards from where they stood talking about the weather, butterflies, and bicycles.

The world had changed for us. Our hearts were still full, but now in a different way than we could have imagined before time stood still. We were no longer blind, but this too was as it should be. Vows spoken on a Thursday in September to become family became reality on a messy, hard evening the following August. Husband and I needed to choose. Stand together, with Father God, or walk apart.

In that moment, God began to sear upon our hearts His goodness and grace, gently whispering into our souls what perhaps we knew all along. Becoming family was so much more than one night of promise and celebration. It was grace, forgiveness, laughter, and tears. It would be listening in silence, laughing loud, holding close, giving forgiveness, sharing hope, and creating memories.

Through the years we began to let God's story be told through our lives. Bits and pieces of hope to others—it was the only way we knew. Our journey to become family was messy and fragmented. It did not fit into a predictable package at the beginning of our marriage nor most places in between.

Sometimes I feel I am holding my breath wondering if we did it right or good enough. However, it is because of Him that there is hope for us, for Baby Girl who became Big Sister to Brother and Little Brother, and for the lives and families they are now creating as adults.

I think this hope of family multiplies and keeps growing. It is not only in the celebrations and parties but also in the darkness and hard places where we make the choice to hold each other close and not let go of those we love no matter what comes.

Husband and I, we are still learning daily what it means to be family, knowing now what we could never have known all along… how precious and priceless the path to becoming family would be.

Nancy Bouwens has been involved in women's ministry for more than 25 years. She has a heart and passion to see women find their place of belonging and purpose at any age and any stage of life. She is a life coach, writer, and empty nester mom to three adult children. She writes and coaches about living a life on purpose for a purpose through intentional choices and by embracing a simpler, slower, and more abundant life.

Nancy has seen the faithfulness of God in the midst of unspeakable pain as her three adult children, within a short seven-month time span, each journeyed through life-changing medical conditions; a car accident resulting from a drunk driver, an auto immune disorder, and a devastating stroke.

She daily holds tight to Psalm 27:13, *"Yet I am confident I will see the LORD's goodness while I am here in the land of the living." (NLT)*

After recently downsizing their life, selling their home of 20 years, and condensing into a much smaller living space, Nancy and her husband, Terry, of 30 years currently make their nest in Grand Rapids, Michigan with Sophie, their four-pound, Yorkshire terrier (who wants to be a Doberman when she grows up). On her current "bucket list" is a hot air balloon ride, dance lessons, experiencing Europe, and visiting every national park in the States. Her favorite travel destination is currently Arizona where her five grandchildren live!

You can find Nancy blogging at www.SimplyAbundantLife.com, via email at nancy@simplyabundantlife.com, on Twitter at @nancy_bouwens, and on Facebook at www.facebook.com/SimplyAbundantLifeCoaching.

The Eager Hostess
By Diana Geisel

There she stood, looking so much like a little girl. Her hopes were clasped in her folded hands in front of her chest. Had she been a little girl, she would have fairly jumped up and down at the sight of us. But she was poised, watching as if praying, "Oh Father, please, please, please can I have visitors?" When she saw us, a smile spread across her face, and she opened the door for us even before we parked the car. She stepped out and greeted us with one of her warmest hugs.

We were late, but that was of no consequence to her. I confessed, "Sorry, Mom, we were late. I had trouble getting away from work."

We were bringing her lunch/dinner. Who eats lunch at 3:00 pm? She waved her hand as if to swish away a fly and announced, "I eat anytime I'm hungry." The pressure of our tardiness dissipated with her proclamation. *How liberating,* I thought. No pressure about the proper time to eat. You just do it when you are hungry. No matter if it is 1:00 pm or 1:00 am.

I quickly entered her apartment, as she had left her door standing open when she went the distance down the hall to the outside door to wait for us. She never worried about intruders. She had nothing of consequence and nothing she worried about losing. She had everything she needed and not too much more, but she was content.

Pictures of her seven children, their spouses, and too many grandchildren to count lined the walls, the piano, the TV hutch, the end tables, the sewing machine table, her bedside stand, and, of course, the refrigerator. Years of Mother's Day sentiments could be found on cups, tea pots, calendars from years gone by, poems in frames and paintings we did as children. Evidence of her life of treasures hanging on the walls and perched on ledges.

Everything was neat and tidy for an 88-year-old woman with eyesight that wasn't so great anymore. She moved about slower than she used to, and she seemed somewhat frail in her movements, but she was still sharp and had a quick wit and sense of humor. She always ate in front of the TV while she watched her religious programming or FOX news.

Today the table was set with a small linen tablecloth. Atop were three plates with three sets of tableware. I popped everything in the microwave to warm for a few minutes, and she started a video for John, my husband, that she had ordered from Newsmax. She sheepishly smiled and said, "I had to subscribe to the magazine to get the DVD on Reagan, and I really wanted the DVD." As it played, John was drawn into it right away as he waited for dinner to be ready.

Mom slowly pulled out a pie tin from the refrigerator as she said, "Guess what I have? Enough pie left over for desert! I made it myself from my own recipe." It looked delicious, and I told her so. She placed that and a Jell-o salad in the middle of the small table. I added a warm pan of chicken and pasta with alfredo sauce and a pan of seasoned green peas next to it.

We sat on three sides of the table, and John reached for my hand and then for hers. She looked up and smiled. Not so used to human touch. He said, "We might not be able to have the honor of holding your hand too much longer. You never know." Then he prayed for the blessing on the meal and those sharing it together.

When we had each had our fill, there was still enough left to leave her with a meal or two for later whenever she was hungry the next time. She proudly brought out her pie and was about to dish out two ginormous pieces when I intervened. "Mom, if you just cut that into three pieces it looks like it would be plenty for all of us." She adjusted her slice size and, sure enough, three nice-sized pieces emerged. She added whipped cream to ours and left her own plain. "Don't you want whipped cream, too, Mom?"

She shook her determined head as she cut her first bite. "No, it's good without." It was good, too.

After the dishes were taken up, she wanted us to just leave them dirty in the sink. I filled the sink with soapy water and said, "I'll just wash these up, then you won't have to later."

She said, "What else am I going to do?" Still I finished them up for her, and she put the food away.

Meanwhile John put a little water and vinegar in a bucket and started to wash her windows. She loved looking out, and she knew her windows could use some cleaning that she was unable to manage herself nowadays. He went to work for her, doing what she could not do for herself, as unto the Lord. He was rewarded by profuse thanks and a genuinely grateful heart.

She showed me some legal paperwork she was having trouble with. I helped her take care of that; I put it in the envelope and filed the copies with her. She sent us home with the Reagan DVD and the Newsmax magazine, puzzles for my grandchildren, and photo paper for my son. She hugged us at the door and walked all the way down the hall again and out to the car with us. More of her wonderful hugs were given. As we drove away, she held up both arms over her head. Using the deaf sign language for "I love you" on both hands she waved them back and forth. As we drove out of her sight, we could still see those raised hands in the rearview mirror.

She was so like a gleeful child and still so like a mother. I hope I will never forget the sight of her waiting for us to arrive and watching us go as we drove out of sight. Somewhere along life's busy path, she was transformed, as we all are, from the stresses and demands of motherhood, to a woman who longed for the sight of her loved ones and delighted in their very presence.

How Decluttering *Transformed* My Life

By Linda Gordon

Slow Transformation

A couple of years ago, I took on a project that began a *transformation* journey in my life. The winter season was approaching, and I was physically and emotionally exhausted from work, home, church, and social responsibilities. Thankfully, the two-week Christmas holiday break was fast approaching. I would be able to get some much needed rest. The first few days of the break were spent on the usual Christmas preparations, and I was able to sleep in, refreshing my physical body. The day after Christmas, I decided to begin the process of decluttering my house – something that would take the remainder of the holiday break.

Twenty-five years of living in the same house and raising three active children had resulted in stacks of papers, piles of clothing, and a plethora of paraphernalia. Years earlier, as a stay-at-home mom, I had been able to maintain a well-run household. As the children went off to school and my husband off to work, I had time and energy to care for our beautiful two-story home. Things had changed, and now I found myself living underneath the weight of clutter.

Where the thought of decluttering came from was a mystery

to me, but I suspect God had something to do with it. Possibly seeds of decluttering had been sown as I often chatted with family and friends about physical clutter in my life. Once my sister, who is a massage therapist, suggested that I might feel physically and emotionally better if I got rid of clutter. She had learned of this concept in a massage therapy class.

My definition of declutter was to get rid of stuff, things that I had not used for years, and things that I would probably never use. For example, hardened Pepto Bismol and expired vitamins congested the bathroom cabinets. Outdated and ill-fitting clothes took up precious space in our small closets. Plastic containers with no lids and severely scratched enamel pots and pans crowded the kitchen cabinets. Dust mites and spider webs were definitely things I never planned to utilize.

I carefully began the decluttering process, starting with the small half bathroom. That went well. From there, I moved on to the full bathroom. All of this took about half a day. From the bathrooms, I moved on to my bedroom, and that is when the magnitude of the task overwhelmed me. It took me two and a half days to declutter a significant portion of my bedroom. Due to the limited amount of days I had for decluttering, I chose to move on to other rooms before completing the bedroom. It was daunting work, but it felt great. I was motivated to forge ahead. Next on my declutter list was the living room, the kitchen, and the den, in that order. I started and partially decluttered each room. My house was slowly being transformed. The Christmas holiday break ended. It was time to return to work.

Health Related Benefits of Decluttering

That first week back at work I felt refreshed and thought to myself, *I really needed that break.* The second week back I felt even better and I was downright happy, almost giddy. I asked myself, *Why are you so happy?* The answer came to me in an instant: *DECLUTTER*. That was the only thing I had done differently. At that moment I recalled the conversation I had with my sister months earlier regarding clutter. She was right. A life transformation had begun.

I was intrigued with the results of freeing my house of stuff and went online to do a little research of my own. There I found a wealth of information on health-related benefits of decluttering. For example, www.inaquandary.co.uk lists the following:

√ *You should be able to sleep better in a clean and tidy environment and spend less time worrying*

√ *You will feel more able to deal with things as and when they happen*

√ *You will feel better equipped to deal with life on a day-to-day basis*

√ *You will have more time to pursue hobbies and outside interests*

√ *Your general health may improve – less colds and flu each year*

√ *You will feel more energized to start projects and see them through to completion*

√ *You will be equipped to part with sentimental items*

The list of benefits was fascinating. Every item on the list affected me to some degree. I was having trouble sleeping soundly at night, and I was often physically sick. Managing life was overwhelming at times, to say the least. I lacked energy on a regular basis and felt that I didn't have enough time in a day for routine tasks, not to mention hobbies or outside interests. The point about being equipped to part with sentimental items spoke volumes to me. At that moment I realized that there were emotions in my past that had been buried underneath clutter.

Buried Under Clutter

While decluttering in the den, I found a desk drawer full of old checkbook stubs. Out of curiosity I began to flip through each one. The dust caused my eyes to itch. This was early 2011, and many of the check stubs dated back to the early 2000's. The deeper I went in the drawer, the older the dates became. At the very bottom of the drawer were check stubs dating back to 1998. That's when it hit me. In 1999, my husband was diagnosed with liver disease, and in 2000 he passed away. I then understood that parts of my life had been put on hold since 1998.

Prior to my husbands' illness and death, I loved being a homemaker. We enjoyed a clean house, a manicured lawn (my husband's hobby), home cooked meals, and wonderful family times. My husband pampered me. Life was good! All of that changed with his passing. In addition to losing my spouse and father of my children, I lost a friend, a lover, a gardener, a handyman, a mechanic, a support system. Now I was a widow with a cluttered house, a working single mother of three with little time and energy to enjoy life. Survival mode had become my new way of living.

Upon making this heart-wrenching discovery, I paused in disbelief. This insight shook me to my core; that's when I understood the power of decluttering. After the Christmas break I continued to declutter at every opportunity. Throughout the process, God began to unveil more of who He had created me to be. With each decluttered drawer, closet, shelf, and room…the drawers, closets, shelves and rooms of my heart were experiencing transformation. A new person was emerging from within, a person whom I liked very much. Life became a bit more enjoyable. I began to live instead of merely survive.

Spiritual Transformation

Several months after my decluttering *transformation* began, I found myself spending the night in a small apartment. I was out of town visiting my sister, and she had a quiet, accommodating space. Her extra apartment was tastefully decorated and had very little furniture. The freshly painted off-white walls were mostly bare. A lush green plant sat in one corner. At one end of the comfortable couch was a small table parallel to the plant. The apartment was situated away from traffic, surrounded by trees. It was her massage studio, a perfect set-up for peace and tranquility.

That summer evening, the atmosphere was warm and freeing. In the apartment, I spent a couple of hours after midnight just hanging out with God, enjoying His presence. There was no clutter to interfere with our intimacy. The next morning, I was gently awakened by nature. I read God's Word, sang praises to His name, and enjoyed the beauty of the outdoors from a window. I didn't want to leave that place. Later, as I pondered and meditated on this experience, the thought occurred to me: *the clutter of things and stuff in our lives breeds idolatry. Things keep us from being transformed into the image of Christ.*

My thoughts continued: *Most of the things that people hold dear are man-made...the house, the furniture, the jewelry, the electronics, the cars, the mall (and all it contains). When we surround ourselves with these things, no wonder we are unable to hear God's still, quiet voice. Unfortunately, most of us surround ourselves constantly, slowly being transformed into the lifeless thing that possesses us, mistakenly thinking that we are living.* This unplanned personal retreat proved to me that, when I am free from the clutters of life, I can experience God in a deeper way.

The Noise of Clutter

Since experiencing the benefits of decluttering and the time at my sister's, I have been on a mission to declutter the remainder of my house. During holiday breaks and some weekends throughout the year, I have managed to take a few hours or a half day for decluttering. Transformation continues to occur, and I am amazed. Something good and exciting is revealed at each juncture. For example, God continued to reveal and free me of other clutter.

Once when I picked up my vehicle from the auto shop after a routine oil change, the radio did not work. I explained to the mechanics that the radio worked when I had dropped off the vehicle that morning. They conducted several tests and found nothing wrong. For the next several months, I traveled to work, went on road trips, and drove back and forth to the grocery store with no radio. Eventually, I began to appreciate this new way of driving. Travel time was now used for prayer and praise to God. *Transformation* from the noise of clutter was taking root.

Several months later, I decided to give up cable television in order to be a better steward of finances. Another blessing in disguise. Almost immediately I did not miss the plethora of annoying commercials, mindless sitcoms, or the negative, nauseating news. By decluttering physical sights and sounds, my *transformation* journey accelerated. The results have been phenomenal; God is increasing, and I am decreasing.

There is a connection between the physical and the spiritual. Having physical things are not wrong, unless we allow those things to interfere with our relationship to God. *"God is spirit and his worshipers must worship in spirit and in truth"* (John 4:24 NIV). In order to commune with our spiritual Father, *transformation* from the clutters of life is necessary. I can testify to this fact because Decluttering Transformed My Life.

Linda Gordon is an inspirational writer. For more than 15 years she has written a one-page newsletter called *The Encourager*, for family and friends. God has used this outreach as a foundation for her current and future writing.

Linda received a BSBA degree from Aquinas College (1981) and graduated summa cum laude from Cornerstone University (2008) with an MSM degree. She is a member of Toastmasters International and Word Weavers International, Inc.

Recently, she completed a nine-month devotional project which transformed her from a mediocre Christian to one who walks in the power of the resurrected Christ. The devotional will be self-published in upcoming months. Linda Gordon resides in Grand Rapids, Michigan.

Home Soon, Come See

By Diana Geisel

Her doctor predicted that her infection would take her life within two days. I shared her care with her dad John, her older brother Rick, and her younger sister Lori. As her mom, I felt I knew her better than I knew myself. We had been together through 28 major surgeries, many mysterious illnesses, several broken bones, and too many medical procedures to count. None of them went easily, and neither she nor I had forgotten that. She seemed to be the medical exception to every rule. Her life expectancy was eight to ten years, but as I would often tell her, "It's not over until God says it's over." When she celebrated her 39th birthday, she proudly announced, "I am now thirty-nine and holding, but I refuse to be forty." What was spoken like a true woman turned out to be prophetic.

Shari had not been well for a very long time. As a matter of fact, when I thought back on it, it was just one year ago from Shari's 39th birthday that she had some undefined infection very similar to the one she had now. Today it was Friday, and I had not heard back from the doctor's office about the tests she had done at the beginning of the week. I paced back and forth, praying for wisdom. My husband and I were scheduled to leave for a vacation to celebrate our anniversary the next week, and I needed to know she was stable if I was to leave her in the care of her sister Lori.

We had thrown a mattress on the floor in the living room so we could respond to her more quickly during the night. She frequently woke with sudden high fever spikes, choking, and retching. Saturday morning she was worse. We agreed that we could not wait for Monday to know what was going on or to start on medication. I approached the subject carefully. "Shari, I think we need to go to the hospital to find out what is going on with you. What do you think?"

She was sick enough that she responded, "I want to know what's wrong, too." We began the process of bathing her, dressing her, brushing out her long hair, and returning it to her favorite hairstyle, a pony tail. After she had eaten very little, we loaded her and her electric wheelchair onto the van's lift and secured her chair to the floor. We headed for the hospital where we knew her doctor had practicing privileges.

Shari was admitted right away and, as usual, getting an IV line into her tiny veins was difficult. The IV did not last beyond the first 24 hours. After several unsuccessful attempts to insert a PIC line, a central line proved to be the last stable line available to get her medication delivered. The antibiotics used were strong, damaging her already compromised kidney function. Shari moaned all through a rough Sunday night but could not put into words what she was feeling. When the lights came on Monday morning, I could see she was retaining fluid and showed obvious swelling in her extremities and abdomen. We were losing the battle. Her doctor entered and sat down on her bed. After praying for us first, he laid out the grim options.

John entered the room, and Shari greeted him with, "Did you hear, Dad? Bad news. I wanted to be thirty-nine and holding but God said, 'Just hold.'" We discussed the options the doctor had outlined for us. It was Shari's decision to make, and she was clear with us. "No more procedures. No more surgery." We looked at each other with a knowing look. For thirty-nine years we had known that this day would come to us. Here we were now at that life crossroad. John questioned her one more time. "Shari, do you understand that this means you will be going to heaven if we do nothing?" She said in a rather determined voice, "No more."

It was her wish to go home and to see her extended family members one more time. We began to call cousins, aunts, uncles, and grandma. Transport arrangements were made. Hospice was called to assist arriving within the hour. By 3:30 pm, she was being transferred by ambulance to her home.

Her sense of equilibrium was so compromised that the ride terrified her. The attendants looked to me for help, and I quickly moved from my seat above her head to the seat directly beside. There, I held her face with one hand and cradled her body in my other arm. She needed to feel the security of my arms around her upper body where I hoped she still had sensation. Her brain deceived her, making her feel as if she was falling. I kept repeating these words, just inches from her face. "You are safe, Baby. Momma's got you. You are locked in. You won't fall. I won't let anything happen to you."

By the time we arrived at the place she loved more than anywhere else in the world, she had already lost the use of her arms and hands. By the time she was settled into her own hospital bed, in her own room, she could no longer speak or swallow. With much instruction and guidance from the Hospice nurse, Lori began administering her medications on a schedule that she and Rick had worked up. The goal was to keep their sister as comfortable as possible.

Very quickly, her breathing became labored. We heard the rattling sounds of pneumonia. To the hospice nurse, it seemed like she had just a matter of hours instead of the two days the doctor projected. Family members began arriving at the house. They came to be with Shari and offer support to the immediate family. They came to witness the last miracles of her life. Her brother, sister, dad, and myself took turns at her bedside through that first night. As the sun came up Tuesday morning, Shari was still with us.

The next night her two aunts said that they wanted to take a shift watching out for Shari as they could see we were all exhausted already. We all agreed that instead of taking shifts of one we would take shifts two by two. So the aunts took the first shift Tuesday night.

Her dad and I went to lay down, a baby monitor stretching through the air waves and connecting her room to ours. We no sooner laid down when the aunts called us. We raced up the steps to find that Shari had suffered a seizure. We touched her hands, stroked her arms and face, and spoke assurance into her ears. "We are here, Shari. We love you. It's OK to go with Jesus when he comes." She settled, and we went back to lie down again. Very soon, we were called again. Another seizure. This time after she settled down we laid ourselves down in recliner chairs in the nearby living room, closer to her room. Once again, we were called. This time, I decided that perhaps God was trying to tell me to stay with her. So I stayed. Her dad would occasionally lie down and come in and out of her room, checking on her.

After awhile as we sat by her bed, both of us thought we heard someone whispering. Looking around, we saw no one. We got up, checked the hall, but there was no one. The whispering continued. It seemed to have a rhythm. We strained to hear the words until I realized that the sound came from the oxygen compressor. It had sounded so real. The rhythm continued, and with it the feeling that God was using this man-made device to deliver a message to me. I prayed silently. "God, please help me hear and understand the words."

Soon I could discern two words repeated at the steady rhythm. "Home Soon...Home Soon...Home Soon. " I turned to her dad. "Can you hear that?" I spoke the words as they seemed to come out of the oxygen machine, matching its rhythm. "Home Soon...Home Soon." He did hear it, but the aunts did not. In fact, they wondered if we were hallucinating. Eventually they moved to our side of the room, and then they heard it too.

Shari suffered one seizure every 10 minutes for an hour or two. Lori called the hospice nurse, and she returned in the middle of the night to stabilize Shari. The seizures stopped. Around 3:30 am, I could no longer sit up. I called Rick from his brief sleep to come and watch for awhile. As I laid myself down, I recalled the words of Christ in the garden before his death. "Could you not watch with me for one hour?" And like the disciples, I wanted to stay but could not hold off sleep any longer. We slept for a short time and at some later hour Rick called us back into her room. Shari's breathing had made a very distinct change, more shallow and quiet. The hospice nurse was with her, helping us to process this change and the meaning of it.

As the sun came up the next morning, family began arriving at the house again. Shari's only living grandparent, her 87-year-old grandma, had stayed by her bedside for the better part of the last three days. She was fulfilling her promise to Shari, that she would not be one of the many people to drift in and out of her life. She would always be there for her.

During that last day, I heard words coming through the air compressor again. The message was different now: I heard "Come See...Come See...Come See." Her dad heard these new words, too. We discerned that God was not speaking to us at all. He was actually speaking to her. In His goodness, He had allowed us to hear Him calling her home, cheering her on. Oh, the things she was about to see upon her arrival at her heavenly home.

We began singing to her as Shari labored for entry into the Kingdom of heaven. Suddenly she frowned big and had a massive seizure, one so great it frightened even the medical veterans standing there. I wept and cried out, "Oh, no, Baby Doll...please, no, not like this." I did not want her end to be one horrible memory. I had been praying for the last three days that God would let us see the wonder and beauty of where she was going through her eyes. We prayed that she would not be afraid. Now it seemed that she was gone. Then suddenly she breathed deeply once again, and I sighed with deep relief. "Thank you, Father."

It was in the early part of the afternoon that we could see her breathing slowing even more. As her sister prepared her next dose of medication, Shari suddenly opened her eyes. Instead of looking up as she had been doing, she was looking at something far away and out the window. She had the slightest smile on her lips. Rick and I both said, "She opened her eyes, and she is seeing something she really likes seeing."John came into the room and bent over her head. "Baby, thank you for all that your life has been teaching me, for all the times I made certain sounds and you told me to say excuse me. Oh, I love you so much." He kissed her head, and she smiled slightly again. Then while we waited for what seemed an endless moment, some began to say, "She's gone." They were right. She was gone at the moment her daddy kissed the top of her head.

At this moment I was oblivious to many of those around me. The person on my right hugged me. My overwhelming thought – the only words that escaped my tongue – were, "She's safe. She's safe."

The presence of the Holy Spirit seemed to rush in and fill the room. Her brother, dad, and others prayed in turn, thankful for the gift He gave us at the end.

This was Shari's transforming moment, but it was mine, too. I had cared for her deformed body, her soul, and her every emotional and spiritual need for 39 years.

Sometimes I thought it might take my own life. Yet we were committed to her. We trusted God to keep us there and together for her. It had transformed our lives, too.

We will never be the same. Now there is no more night for her, for the Lamb is the light. "Behold I show you a mystery; we shall not all sleep, but we shall all be changed...for this mortal (body) must put on immortality..." I Corinthians 15:51 (KJV)

I Hope He'll Come Home

By Teresa K. Lasher

"When they're little, they pull on your apron strings. When they grow older, they pull on your heart strings." – Anonymous

My pillow felt lumpy. I slept with my wallet and any valuables under it to prevent being robbed by our son. I glanced over at my husband as he snored. *How can he possibly be asleep?*

Where had our teenage son Andy disappeared to this time? When would we hear from him—or the authorities—again? He hadn't made contact with us for several days. My mind, body, and soul grew weary of phone calls from upset teachers, principals and department store security officers. Our lives were much more complicated now. I barely knew the school and church friends he hung out with. Occasionally, Andy would mention a first name—if I probed. Embarrassment and fear were our steady companions.

I prayed for a phone call from anyone regarding his whereabouts. We would gladly come rescue him wherever he had roamed. It didn't matter; we just wanted our son back. If only I had a clue that he was safe and alive, I could rest easier. My mind conjured up horrible images of him being stuck in a snowbank head first without identification and no way to track him back to us.

Slow down. Take deep breaths. *Oh, God, you know the beginning from the end. I need to remember that You love Andy exceedingly more than we could ever love him. You created him and won't allow anything we cannot handle.*

Finally, I drifted asleep still keeping an ear open for the closure of a door or window. Just knowing family and friends covered us in prayer relieved my mind temporarily. There were many times when I couldn't even utter a prayer.

Jeremiah 29:11–14 became a favorite passage I returned to again and again:

"For I know the plans I have for you," declares the Lord, "plans to prosper you and not to harm you, plans to give you hope and a future. Then you will call on me and come and pray to me, and I will listen to you. You will seek me and find me when you seek me with all your heart. I will be found by you," declares the Lord, "and will bring you back from captivity."

Knowing that God stands sentry over my life and the life of my precious children (and future grandchildren) grants certain solace. All I have to do is call. God listens to my cries—especially the cries from a desperate heart. The call doesn't have to be a long eloquent preacher-type prayer. He hears my simplistic SOS longing plea to be heard and found by the God of the universe.

I believe that when I seek God sincerely with all my heart, I will find him. It's God's promise. He rescues and brings me back from captivity—held in bondage by fears and doubts. I will never give up praying and loving my child unconditionally. I desperately prayed Andy would be found by someone before he ended up dead in a snow bank, in a car accident, or under the influence of alcohol or drugs. He was God's creation, fearfully and wonderfully made (Psalm 139). I was his mother and would not give up on him as long as I had breath left in me.

* * * * *

While I had been reading a Bible story to our children, Andy had once asked if he could ask Jesus into his heart. Andy was four years old and his sister only three. We bowed our heads in prayer thanking God for sending his son Jesus to the earth to pay for our sins. Then he asked Jesus to come into his heart and life. His sister prayed the same prayer. To know both of our children now had the assurance of salvation and eternal life made for a most memorable night!

I remember one vacation we spent together on a 22-foot sailboat sloop, sailing from port to port. Andy and his sister, ages five and six, behaved well and played together like best friends. I never understood how that worked since we traveled in a boat smaller than one of their bedrooms at home.

Andy and his younger sister could barely wait until we landed at the dock to jump off the boat, fishing poles in hand, and commence fishing. Their goal was to catch the biggest or most fish. We required them to wait until all lines were firmly attached to the dock before they disembarked.

My husband and I adjusted dock lines and then began preparations for dinner. All of a sudden, Andy ran to me and whispered, "Mom, can I tell you a secret?"

"Of course, you can. What is it?"

"I told that boy about Jesus!" He pointed to another young boy standing on a dock several piers over from us. Nothing could thrill a mom's heart more than to learn her excited child felt comfortable enough to share Jesus and his faith with a total stranger.

That's just the way Andy was as a child—tenderhearted and compassionate toward others. He was the one who came to me and placed his hand in mine even when children at that age had given up hand-holding.

As I think back to those tender moments, I ask myself—how could this happen to a family who attended church? And not just on Sundays either, but on Wednesday for Boy's Brigade and Pioneer Girls. We brought our children to their age-appropriate Sunday school morning classes where they learned about Jesus and memorized scripture. Together we were involved in church and school choir, drama programs, and music lessons. How could these things happen to families like ours? I didn't have the answers, but I had plenty of questions.

Tears came easily during Andy's wandering years. It was all I could do to get out of bed in the morning, shower and dress to face the day. Unknown to me at the time, I was the one being transformed from the inside out, and I was the one who needed changing. I learned to rely daily on God, not on my own feeble strength. God proved that He can be depended on during big crises and in the small details in life.

I prayed. I cried. I prayed some more. Wasn't I there when Andy said his first words and took that first step? Surely, I knew him better than anyone. As his mother, I had dreamed about, carried, and nurtured him for nine long months in my womb. Still, my job was to let go and let God take care of my son in His way and in His perfect timing. God knew ahead of time about Andy's propensity to wander. He knew how much his mother and father loved their son. God knew about the pain and suffering. None of this came as a surprise to the gracious, loving Heavenly Father.

God was still in the driver's seat even though circumstances didn't look that way. Doing things my way was not what God intended. He asked me to trust and obey Him even in the midst of my world caving in. I opened my clenched fists and raised them toward heaven. *Your will—not mine, Lord.*

Our family survived many trials and attempts to restore the family. Thankfully, God has a way of replenishing those broken dreams and lives. He's good at that. When I try to fix things, I often botch it up, but He doesn't.

One of the toughest decisions we ever made was to enlist our teenage son into a long-term residential care facility hundreds of miles from our home. Giving up our rights and relinquishing total care to strangers nearly broke our hearts. We shed many tears going back and forth to visit him four states away. God knew this move was for the best. It was at Minnesota Teen Challenge where our son claims, "The Holy Spirit got ahold of me and wouldn't let go!"

I am thrilled to report that our son re-committed his life to the Lord and now lives in obedience to God. And the blessings continue to unfold: Andy's been married for thirteen years and has owned his own business for four years. In fact, Andy and his wife recently welcomed their fourth child into the world. Four grandchildren...compared to a time when I didn't know when (or if) I'd see my son again. His dad and I are as pleased as any parents could possibly be.

I, too, am not that same person who lived in fear of what would become of our first-born child. Now when frightening situations arise that could cripple me with worry or doubt, I remember back to the time when God did not leave us alone.

Our Heavenly Father provided for us exceedingly above what we could ever ask or think. Now, we sleep comfortably at night, and my pillow is less lumpy than it used to be!

Teresa Lasher is a wife, mom, nana (grandma), brain tumor survivor, and follower of the Lord Jesus Christ. Her passion is encouraging and affirming the stressed to live in and enjoy the present moment.

She was born in Iowa, but moved around (not always willingly) to four different states while growing up. Teresa attended two different high schools — a challenging task for a newbie in a strange town and state. Somehow she landed in Michigan where she met and married her high-school sweetheart. Two children, four grandchildren and over 30 years later, Teresa and her husband Steve still reside in the Great Lake state of Michigan, enjoying beautiful lakes and trails.

Teresa enjoys reading all genres of books, writing devotionals and non-fiction works about boating or motorcycle travels. Walking outdoors in nature's beauty is her favorite get-away — particularly near water. She LOVES spending any amount of time with her children, grandchildren, extended family, and friends.

Her blog, *Living in the Present*, began just after hospitalization for removal of a brain tumor. Sections from the blog appear in her current book project where she shares reflections about proper self care of the mind, body, and soul. Come visit her blog at: www.teresalasher.com/blog.

Motherhood Musings

By Sally Stap

Motherhood is a dance of holding on, letting go, and changing. It takes us from one "just getting comfortable" phase to the next–sometimes at an uncomfortable rate of speed. Through the humble role of motherhood, we begin to understand God's love for us as we develop a mother's love for our children. We begin to comprehend the concept of love conveyed in Psalm 36:5 (NIV), "Your love, Lord, reaches to the heavens, your faithfulness to the skies." Our hearts soar as well as break through connections that intertwine our souls for life.

Having children taught me that my heart can hear. Listening to my children's needs, many times at the cost of my own selfish desires, taught me to give. I learned that motherhood is like a cable with many overlapping, fibrous cords. Throughout each pregnancy, the cable formed, tightly wound and thick. At birth, the intertwined fibers began the gradual process of breaking, snapping, and stretching. The first cut was that of the umbilical cord. It didn't hurt physically, but when my babies were literally cut from my body, we lost the connection that held us together for nine months of planning, dreaming, and bonding. It would be some time before I would recognize and understand that sound of fibers breaking in my heart.

When I met my first daughter, I already loved her more than trees have leaves in summer. I loved her more than my arms could hug her tiny body. I loved her more than all the kisses I could plant on her precious, soft cheeks. Her newborn smile lit up my heart and brought joy to my soul. I still remember holding her when she was only a few minutes old. Her tiny face opened a door in my life and a corner in my heart that I didn't know was there. Watching her sleep, holding her newborn body on my shoulder, and even changing her diaper made me want to protect her forever. However, that was not to be. As I dreamed of what I wished for her life, I could only pray for God's hand to lead her.

I committed to praying for her each day, month, and year. I prayed that her steps would strengthen as her spirit found direction. I asked that she would develop humor, kindness, and compassion for others in her heart. I prayed that she would make wise choices in life, decisions and convictions that would find her principled and honest in character. I prayed that she would become a Godly woman. I knew that as much as I loved her, our God loved her even more. I committed to cheer her successes even as I resolved to share her losses.

Letting my little baby cry herself to sleep in a big crib, in a big room, almost ripped my heart out. I felt another fiber tearing as I walked into the hall and quietly closed the door behind me, burying my face into my husband's chest. We both agreed that it was for her best, but my heart questioned that wisdom. Before the night was out, I felt complete again as I gazed through the window at the bluish moon while in the nursery rocking chair, holding her tightly in my arms as she suckled at my breast. I believe my heart could hear the soothing sound of a cord healing, its fibers pulling tight. I learned I just wasn't ready for some fibers to break.

After a year of carrying her everywhere and looking forward to her first steps, she finally learned to walk. When she took those first wobbly steps away from me, teetering toward someone else, my heart not only soared with pride but also hurt. As I foresaw the future, I began to recognize the sensation in my heart as yet another cord broke free.

I wondered how I could possibly love a second child as much as I did the first. However, as my second daughter entered my world, I learned that "as much" was not an issue. Loving each child differently but entirely taught me how to be flexible. I understood how God can truly love and understand each of us as we traverse life. I understood how He knows and cares for us individually, as we learned through Jesus' parable: "Suppose one of you has a hundred sheep and loses one of them. Doesn't he leave the ninety-nine in the open country and go after the lost sheep until he finds it? And when he finds it, he joyfully puts it on his shoulders and goes home. Then he calls his friends and neighbors together and says, 'Rejoice with me; I have found my lost sheep'" (Luke 15:4-6, NIV).

I prayed for my babies, leaning on God to help position them where they needed to be in this world. When holding each small, soft hand, I visualized the day they would be taller than I. In my heart, I saw their futures even before they were tomboys and girly girls. I saw them as teenagers, tall and lean, rolling their eyes at me, "Yes, Mom, I'll get to the dishes." I saw them as grown women, confident in themselves as they ventured into the world. I trusted that they would each find a path that was right for them.

My kids were always the cutest children in the world as I watched them learn their own preferences in life. I loved daily rituals like watching *Mr. Rogers* and *Reading Rainbow*. One day, I felt another fiber slip away when the youngest said she didn't like those shows anymore and wanted to watch something else. I wanted to protest because I had become quite attached to Mr. Rogers. I learned that motherhood meant I had to let go of things that initially seemed silly. I had to transition away from activities that I had learned to enjoy and had looked forward to sharing. Moving from one experience of letting go to the next, motherhood is adapting to what my children need, not what I want.

I loved sitting while my daughters tugged and pulled at my hair, putting in ten barrettes and six ponytails. I found delight in spending time with my daughters as they grew, and I marveled at their logic and wit as they figured out that the cat should be named Pickle because his eyes were green. I treasured every minute that we spent painting fingernails in the living room while watching movies. Sometimes motherhood is baking cookies while listening to a school day's activities. Other times it's folding laundry while laughing about a silly joke.

Sending the first off to college was tough. However, walking to my car after settling the youngest in her dorm room was downright startling. The transformation to an empty nest was deafeningly quiet. I learned how to do less laundry, have no school events to attend, and buy less food. I learned to manage the remote control, watching whatever I wanted.

When the eldest got her first apartment, I flashed back to my first apartment. As I had navigated an uneven flow of boxes and furniture, excited about unpacking, my mother hopped out of her car and into the kitchen with bags of groceries. It hadn't occurred to me that I would need food, and I had no clue how to cook it. I made sure my daughters had cupboards full of food in their first apartments. As that cord broke when I drove away, I felt satisfied that this generation had fulfilled its obligation. I recognized that my mother and I shared similar cords, perhaps just blended differently.

When my daughters called with questions about education, career, or their hearts, more cords were stressed to the breaking point. Depending on the subject, I had to determine if it was time to talk reality or be an idealist. *No, these are times to just listen,* said my heart. They were now adults needing a sounding board. I learned to cherish and cling to the remaining cords.

My daughters became engaged and then married. Oh, how my heart tightened as I saw them each make lifetime vows to the men in their lives. I prayed for wisdom to carry them through life's pleasures, adversities, and day-to-day life. A big cord let go on their wedding days.

The major life lesson I learned as a mother is that there is one permanent, resilient cord between mothers and children. Whether a child is born from our bodies or bonded through a first touch leading to adoption, a cord is formed. Just like our relationship with God, the cord between mother and children stretches and then springs back intermittently. Cords are stretched to points where we don't feel needed anymore as our children become adults. However, we are bonded for life, and even physical distance cannot break this bond. This connection demonstrates to us how we will never be separated from God. "For I am convinced that neither death nor life, neither angels nor demons, neither the present nor the future, nor any powers, neither height nor depth, nor anything else in all creation, will be able to separate us from the love of God that is in Christ Jesus our Lord" (Romans 8:38-39, NIV).

Motherhood brought awareness of who I am as a daughter, transforming my identity once again. I became flooded with a new knowledge of what my mother went through for me. Birthdays weren't just special days for me, but for her also. I became heart-aware of how my actions brought her joy, pain, or worry. Each phase of motherhood brought to light a longstanding, but perhaps unnoticed, cord between us.

As our children become adults, we grieve even as we celebrate. Upon reflection, we realize we were surprisingly successful at producing self-sufficient children. We move on and pick up our lives, somewhat stunned, to search for who we were, or are, or want to be as our identity as mothers become smaller.

Then, just as we are stabilizing in this new world, when we least expect it, that cord springs back, and we are needed in an instant. We need to be ready anywhere, anytime, without question, to provide what our children need. We might grumble outwardly at the interruption, but our hearts are delighted and joyful to be needed. We hear the cord singing in recoil as we spring back into their lives for however long they will need us.

I have learned as a mother that God loves us immeasurably. He loves us completely. There is nothing that can separate us from Him. He is and was and will forever be. We can be still and bask in His love and light. Motherhood transforms our understanding of what's important.

And then there's the grandchildren....

Sally Stap lives near family in Kalamazoo, Michigan. During a successful Information Technology career, she published magazine articles on outsourcing and pharmaceutical regulatory issues. She spent a considerable part of her career interpreting information technology jargon for business organizations. When that life path was halted by a brain tumor, she shifted to writing in the hope that her experiences will bring reassurance and inspiration to others. Writing brings her pleasure when the right words are found to capture what we all live and feel. While traversing brain surgery recovery, she learned to laugh at herself, discovering that a sense of humor helps brings more joy than frustration.

Sally is a member of the Kalamazoo Christian Writer's critique group as well as the Word Weavers and FaithWriters organizations. She is the author of the book *Smiling Again: Coming Back to Life and Faith after Brain Surgery*. She is also the author of the essay *Laundry*, which was included in *Imagine This! An ArtPrize Anthology*. Her website is www.smilingagainbook.com.

A New Game

By Darlene Lund

Writing was way out of my league. Three strikes had left the message, *stay away from writing.* Burrowing into my safe, mental dugout, I chose not to take the risk of writing until double deaths delivered a wake-up call.

The backdrop for strike one was English 101, my freshmen year college course. I wrote with flair and sprinkled in fun with a creative punch. After all, I had won the creative writing award my senior year in high school. In fact that was my favorite class my senior year, and my teacher created a safe field for writing. I tossed words out on paper as if I were pitching for a major league baseball game.

However, my college professor thought otherwise. Week after week, he handed my papers back with his red checkmarks and scribbling. Oh, I tried so hard to write to his specifications. Each paper handed back reinforced the message, *you are out of the writing game. In fact, you can't even get to first base.* Then he called for a time out. Dreading and slouching, I arrived at his office to review my messed-up work. I knew then that I was in serious need of learning how to write *differently.* I improved just enough to pass the course.

Deflated, I decided I liked writing, but the ability to write was not a part of my future game. The defeat from the negative messages left me a reminder. My red-pen paper comments would not be all negative when I became a K-8th grade teacher. I desired my students to pick up a pencil or pen and not be kicked out of the writing game. I held to that promise.

However, that college course left its ugly residue of impossible thinking in my mind, and for my remaining college years I hated the word "research" and dreaded term papers. But I persevered and obtained my degree.

The second strike arrived a few years after completing college. It was change-over time. Computers were coming off the conveyor belt, and I switched from handwriting to the keyboard. Quite proudly, I sent out my first computer-generated letter to an admired missionary friend. Her response grieved me to the core. "You've lost your compassionate voice in the typing."

Those words stunned and shocked me. I wrestled with her statement. I didn't believe I had lost my compassionate voice. Empathy was a part of my make-up.

So what caused the second strike? Was it the lack of confidence with using a machine instead of a pen that caused my compassionless, computer-generated letter, or was it the other piece in my story that was beginning to gnaw and grind me down? Or maybe it was both?

Yet I made a choice. If my writing was going to come across without any compassion, I would rather deny the reader a story.

The third strike was the costliest and longest lasting. It left a deep scar. At times, it still welts a bit as the healing continues. This strike was delivered by a trusted loved one. "You can't write. You give too much detail. You need to write differently." That stymied my writing, and my fear of inadequacy grew.

Twenty years later, death arrived up close and personal—not one, but two deaths. No warning signs, no goodbyes, just suddenly gone. I faced the deep loss of my father and my brother within three years. I allowed the horrific pain to penetrate my inner being, forcing me to take inventory of my life. Viewing my youngest sibling in a casket was heart-wrenching. It seemed so wrong. Don't we silently assume we will go out in birth order? Not so.

If that were me lying there in that casket, what legacy would I leave? My answer jolted my foundation. I was dynamited out of my denial. I groaned and grieved. If that were me in the casket, I would leave a false message about my adult years. Oh, I groveled in pain. Death had silenced my brother's voice. He no longer had a choice. Fear had silenced my voice. Yet, I had a choice. I was *still* alive.

I shifted. Determined to recapture my voice no matter the fallout, I headed back to the field of writing. It felt as if a bag of bats was strapped around my legs, forcing me to sit and learn at that dinosaur of a desktop. This was challenging. But I could learn.

During this warm up time with the computer, I also addressed other "issues and players" in my life such as anger, manipulation, betrayal, deception, repetitive rejection, and bullying. These were all turning points that caused me to investigate and take action. I needed to discover the answer to the question, *Why am I even still alive?* God being a God of truth, He led me down the road of self-discovery in exposing the pretense in my story. It took days, weeks, months, and years to get my feet stepping forward. And my life turned around in a new direction. With His leading, transformation occurred.

One of my many steps involved seeking a writing coach. I also attended writing conferences. I met publishers. I wrote a monthly newsletter and a coaching column. Online devotionals became my first outlet for writing. I continued to write, edit, re-write, and submit stories for publication. Planting myself in a chair was challenging, as it was polar opposite of my style. But I wrote. Articles were sent off for editing, and I told myself, "You can write." I did write. I spoke truth.

My heart shifted. Writing became a positive event. My love for writing was rekindled as the words began to dance on the page and create momentum. The words flowed as I wrote truth to speak to the hearts of women. I challenged women to investigate where they were on their journey, with purposeful living for their Creator.

Another shift occurred. I chose to address that curveball of a word called *research* that I had so hated in college. I changed out *research* for *harvest*. I now *harvest* information. I glean and gather. *Harvest* is a better fit for me since I am a farmer's daughter. The word produced positive pictures from my mind's memory bank instead of negative images that *research* stirred up. Plus, when using *research,* I felt as if the writing process would be a never-ending drudgery. With *harvest*, there comes an ending, just like in a ball game the completion of the task or innings and the positive, productive feeling of accomplishing a job. My feelings matched when I completed and submitted my very first story for publication, hoping it would be selected for a coaching book.

The author of the coaching book had selected and challenged thirty-two coaches to write an article but to stay away from the first chapter's topic on fear. She believed most of us would write on that. Well, I knew my story fit that chapter like a glove. Fear had been my enemy, yet I knew it like my best friend. But I heeded her advice. I wrote out my story and wrapped it under one of the other chapter titles in the book, *Learn to Exhale*. Yet, down deep, I knew better. Fear had been my tag-along for too many years.

Finally, I received an email about my submission. Tears of joy fell. The author desired I resubmit my story. This time she wanted me to write it so it would go under the chapter on fear. The story is in the coaching book *Live Big* by Dr. Katie Brazelton.

The desire to teach through the written word continues to grow and multiply. My voice is getting stronger and louder. Typing with a voice of compassion, I am hitting line drives daily.

I am passionate to teach and encourage women in the Truth. A long time ago, I envisioned speaking to and teaching women. But then I suspected I would be speaking about how to do the Christian living thing *the right way and perfectly*.

More than thirty years later, I smile because I know I am speaking from a woman's heart that was betrayed, bruised, and battered through life experiences, so I'll leave off the word *perfectly*. I can guarantee most women would not have waited in line to sign up for my life. God is still in the business of redeeming brokenness, and He is transforming a wounded woman to become more than a conqueror through Jesus.

So I finally get it. The three go together: teaching, speaking, and writing. What a trio. It's His call to me. "Coach women. Then speak, teach, and write for audiences of women."

It's a new ball game. I step up to the plate. I write. I learn the craft. I write with compassion, even on a computer. And I anticipate several home runs.

Darlene Lund is a Life Purpose Coach® and Grief Loss Coach, working toward her certification as a Recovery Coach for Women. She is a catalyst, inspiring others to change and experience spiritual transformation.

She is founder of Hearts with a Purpose, which allows women to unpack their life stories through coaching, courses, life-plans, and grief-plans which then empowers them to step forward with purpose. Coaching, speaking, teaching, and writing moves Darlene forward on her own purposeful pathway.

Visit www.heartswithapurpose.com to sign up for a monthly newsletter, sample a coaching session, or to contact Darlene for coaching and/or request her as a speaker for your women's event.

Darlene is co-author of *Submersed in the Secret Sorrow of Infertility*, a self-discovery workbook offering hope to women. She contributed part of her story in the coaching book *Live Big* by Dr. Katie Brazelton. She is a mom to three young adults and a grandmother of one of the world's greatest granddaughters.

The Open Hand
By Diana Giesel

I sat next to her while she fought to absorb the news that her brain cancer was terminal. She was only forty-three years old, and she homeschooled her two children. She struggled with how things would continue for her family after she was gone. Suddenly she looked at me. Rising off her bed, she twisted so she could see me better. Her eyes looked deeply into mine. "Mom, you may have to move into my house."

"I have thought about it, Diane, and I want you to know that we will do whatever it takes. I promise."

She relaxed back on her bed and closed her eyes. As she did, I bowed my head and recalled to mind the first conversation I'd had with Diane's husband – my son Rick – about her health.

It was Mother's Day, 2012. I was having a coveted lunch alone with Rick to celebrate. I casually asked him how his wife Diane was doing. He responded, "Actually, there is something that we are looking into and have not identified yet. She doesn't think it is anything to worry about and doesn't really want to talk about it."

My eyes lifted from my salad and met his. "What's going on, Rick?"

He began to explain what he could only describe as short

spells. He said, "I haven't actually seen it myself, but she describes it like this: She will be frozen for a few seconds and, after it has passed, seems not to be aware of what had happened during that time. She seems to know something is about to happen and says she just feels like she needs to sit down."

Not wanting to alarm him, I said, "My immediate thought is that she could be having some kind of seizure." In my mind that translated into the fear, that this was something related to her brain.

Rick continued. "Diane did go to her doctor for a checkup, and she had something slightly unusual with her EKG. The doctor wanted her to wear an event heart monitor for a time. Diane has put off wearing it since we are about to leave for Virginia to see her family."

To me, this was potentially serious and needed to be taken seriously. I exclaimed in shock. "Rick, you need to get right on top of this. We can't lose Diane."

Suddenly how irreplaceable she was became clear and caused me to shudder. I conceded that putting this monitor idea off was a reasonable request on Diane's part. She just wanted to go on vacation and not have to carry around the constant reminder that she had a possible health issue looming. She just wanted to enjoy her family and her time at the ocean.

* * * * *

While at the beach everyone noticed that Diane went to bed and consistently awoke with a headache. Headaches had been a part of Diane's life. So while there was nothing new about her having occasional headaches, there was an indescribable undercurrent of concern over the frequency.

Diane's mother Juanita expressed her opinion on these health issues. "Diane, I think you should have a CAT scan or an MRI."

Upon her return from Virginia, she wore the event monitor,

which showed no heart irregularities. Her headaches increased, and she found herself unable to sleep since they worsened during the night.

The undefined episodes became more frequent and slightly more concerning. Diane would often pace the floor at night and cry. It was not typical for her to call me about her illnesses or complaints. She was very stoic – a woman who suffered in private. That's why I took her very seriously when one day in the middle of the week, she called crying. She told me her mother wanted her to have an MRI.

"Diane, I do, too. I agree with your mom."

When Sunday came around, we often had dinner after we all attended church together. It was Diane's custom to take our handicapped daughter, Shari, for a week each month to give us a break from the physical difficulty of her care. So after dinner it was natural that she began to discuss with me the issues that surrounded taking Shari. She was thinking about our schedules.

I looked straight into the windows to her soul. "Diane, not this time. I really think you need to get to the bottom of what's going on with these spells first."

She returned my gaze and tried to reassure me that it was nothing. I think we both knew better somehow.

It was over my lunch break from my home desk job the next week that the phone rang again. It was a beautiful day and, as I took the call, I walked out onto the deck.

Again I heard the tears as Diane described her sleepless nights to me and her fear over an upcoming chiropractor appointment she had scheduled that day. She cried quietly into the phone. "I feel like I am dying."

"I hear you, Diane.

"Why don't you cancel that appointment if it feels upsetting to you? Call your doctor and tell her that your symptoms have changed. See what she recommends."

She quieted her crying and sniffed. "I will."

An appointment was made with the doctor, and an MRI was scheduled right away. The day of the MRI, Rick had prearranged for his dad John to take the kids to their soccer game. I was at work at my office.

The doctor had asked Rick and Diane to wait for the results after the MRI.

The technician entered the waiting room. They were a little alarmed when she directed them to return to the doctor's office immediately.

* * * * *

At his office, the doctor came in and took a seat across from them. "Something significant was seen on your MRI," she said. "I want you to go back to the MRI testing center and pick up your films and reports. Head straight to the hospital emergency room. I have called ahead, and they are expecting you.

"We don't know for sure what we are seeing, but it could be one of three things. It could be cancer, MS, or an infectious disease process. The affected area could produce seizures, so we need you to get to the hospital as soon as you have picked up the MRI films."

The doctor gave them a minute to themselves.

Rick put his head in Diane's lap and sobbed.

Ever the caretaker, Diane smoothed his hair and comforted him. "It will be okay, Rick." He was there to give her support, and there she was comforting him instead.

Rick called to alert me to this unforeseen change of events, and I could hear the unspoken concern in his voice.

I asked, "Rick do you want me to come?"

His voice broke as he simply said, "Yes."

Now I knew something was seriously wrong. I called John

and asked him to stop at the house and pick up some extra clothes for the kids. We were going to plan on the kids being with us overnight, at least a day or two.

After loading our daughter, Shari, into the van, I met John. He would take Shari and exchange vehicles with me.

* * * * *

After many tests, several specialist teams converged to look at the test results. Eventually, it was suspected that Diane had brain cancer of some type. The cancer specialist described two or three masses and said, "It looks like someone just threw sugar all over your brain. That is rather unusual. We don't usually see something like that."

Surgery and biopsies would be needed to be absolutely sure of this diagnosis.

* * * * *

After surgery, the doctor took Rick, Juanita, and me into a separate room. He delivered the news that this was a very aggressive form of brain cancer called Glioblastoma Multiforme.

"This is a cancer that originates in and stays in the brain. The prognosis is three months to three years at best. Realistically, very few survive to the three-year mark.

"The most serious tumors are inoperable."

Rick reached out to take hold of the doctor's hand. "I know this was hard news to deliver. Thank you for your honesty and your expert care for Diane."

We asked a few questions as we all tried to absorb what was just said.

When the surgeon left the room, he invited us to stay as long as we needed.

We huddled together, holding each other as we wept. We wept for Diane and Rick, whose twenty year marriage anniversary would soon be celebrated. We wept for the children, ten-year-old Grace, and twelve-year-old Gideon.

It would be Rick's job to give them the devastating news. It would be my job to deliver the news to everyone else in the waiting room, eager to know what we had been told.

* * * * *

During the weeks that followed, a treatment plan was laid out. A rescue trip to Duke University Cancer Treatment Center was planned but to no avail. Upon her arrival, Diane was so unstable that she was hospitalized the very first day.

The cancer had done what it rarely does. It had spread to her spinal fluid. The world-renowned team of doctors said that, if they could not help her, they would send her home. For the time being, they did not want her leaving the hospital or going back and forth to Michigan.

* * * * *

When Rick's name appeared on my caller ID, I quickly answered the call. As I listened to Rick's account of what had already transpired, I could hear the emotion mounting and sensed that he was conflicted.

"Is there anything that we can do, Rick?"

He spilled out his fears. "I am concerned that the kids will never see their mom again if we can't come home."

Based on the seriousness of her condition upon her arrival – and now this added news – it seemed a virtual certainty that Rick's fear for the children was well-founded.

"Rick, what if we bring the children to you? Dad and I could drive them down and stay for however long you think it wise for them to be there, for you to have them there."

By the weekend all the arrangements were made for time off. We had found someone to care for Shari, too.

As we started our road trip to North Carolina, I was on the phone with my sister. She had come to be with my mom in my place, as Mom had just entered the hospital with congestive heart failure.

My mother, my daughter Shari, and my son's family tore my heart in three different directions. "Father, please hold me together."

* * * * *

Diane was losing ground quickly, but she was glad to see her children when we arrived. The worst possible news awaited us at every turn. Only a week after we got to Duke, we heard the news that the doctor was sending us all home.

Diane looked at Rick and said, "Did I just get a death sentence?" She seemed to understand that we all needed to get back to Michigan before anything else happened. She worked hard to meet the criteria for her release from the hospital so we could get home. We strategized about what we would do if something happened along the way and where we would stop for the night. We drove fast until we reached home.

It was just three weeks later that Diane lost her ability to walk and stand. An ambulance was called to transport her back to the local hospital. After evaluation, we were advised that it was time for Hospice to step in.

Finally, we took the solemn trip to the Hospice House, where Diane would live out her remaining days.

On the last evening I saw her, I bent over her body to say goodbye to her. She could no longer speak to me, and these would be the last words I spoke to her. I whispered in her ear. "Diane, thank you for all you did for our family. Thank you for all you did for me.

"Thank you for loving my son. Thank you for being such a good mom. We won't do it as good as you did, but we will do our best to take care of the children.

"I promise you this. I will love your children until death parts us. It's okay to go with Jesus when He comes. I love you."

Diane died in the early morning hours of September 29, 2012. Life would never be the same for any of us.

* * * * *

There is so much untold story between these lines.

We would soon approach our first Christmas without Diane.

The Christmas season was marked with the love and beauty that only comes in the wake of deep sorrow and loss. It caused us to reflect too deeply and to feel the pain too profoundly and to find ourselves too weak to move ahead at times. It was then that we agonized in prayer to a God who does care and who has a plan that He would be working out and that we would be honored to be part of.

The challenge of that Christmas still runs through my mind. Could we open our hands and know that, whether the plan hurts or brings pleasure, His plan for us was good?

Sometimes what is good comes with pain. Sometimes blessings come to us as something hard.

The trials of 2012 came suddenly – like a Tsunami – one huge wave. A benign spell. Increasing headaches. Bad news. Cancer.

God called our precious loved one away from suffering, away from this broken world, and to Himself. He called her to His world of peace, beauty, music, clean air and water, pure motives, and a spotless life.

We are happy for her. We are grieved for the entire family, our extended family, and hers.

She declared that she had learned from each of us things that she would not have come to know without us. And we each learned from her life, too. She left us each with a mandate to never quit doing what God had called and gifted us to do for His glory and His purposes. We were honored to have her for 20 years and to bear witness to her life, her growth and her passage to Heaven.

Diane had begun the work of seeing God's gifts in the small and plentiful things all around us. She let go of her own plans, her own desires, her own way, her own time, her own schedule. She gradually cultivated a heart of gratitude. She showed this in the amazing and graceful way she suffered. Then she let go of her temporary life.

It is the transformation we are all called to make. For we will all let go of life, whether we cling hard to it or submit to letting it go with hands open to God's will. Though the temptation could have been there to be angry or make deals with God, Diane did not succumb to it. Even when she could no longer speak, she raised her hand in praise to God, and in submission to His will, knowing that He is the resurrection and the Life. She wanted to get this one last thing right.

For Diane, every day is Christmas now. Every day is a day that Diane can remember what God did when He sent His Son Jesus Christ to do for us what we could never do for ourselves. Every day she knows the joy of being fully alive.

May we each discover the joy of living our one life in gratitude and praise and thanks for all that God has left for us to discover all around us, as we carry on.

Mikhail

By Maria De Lugt Kocsis

When Mikhail was half-sober, he might caress or pound the keys of his piano, depending on his mood. His command of those keys, full of feelings both light and dark, touched my soul.

Mikhail had come to America years before with his Russian wife, a very stern-looking woman. She had needed a kidney transplant, something she could not get in Russia. So they immigrated to America. Mikhail worked as a professional musician and a ballet society director while his wife studied at the university. After she graduated, she divorced him. She had said she could no longer tolerate his drunken outbursts.

My sister Jo met Mikhail after he held a concert at her church in Westerville, Ohio. She telephoned me afterwards.

With great excitement, she told me that I just *had* to come to their next concert. She explained that Mikhail had performed on the piano, accompanying a Russian violinist. As Jo described it, their playing could make you weep. Following her advice, I made it a point of attending their next performance. I was every bit as enthralled with their talents as my sister had been.

At the time, Jo had served as the church organist. Over the years, she would share her talent for encouraging, influencing, and even cajoling Mikhail to accompany her on the piano for the morning services.

He was not a Christian, but he felt a kinship to Jo and seemed to want to please her. And so he played in the venues she would approve of. She beamed like a mother, marveling at the talents of a son. In turn, he routinely addressed her as "Mama."

This man, a former Russian soldier, was a very private person. One might describe him as introverted. Or guarded. Or hard. Yet my sister had found a way to break through his protective shell, using music as her tool.

Mikhail would come to Jo's house regularly for dinner. Since it usually took him a few minutes to come in, Jo began watching him from her kitchen window. She was dismayed to find that he would take a few swigs from a booze bottle kept in his car before walking up to the door. After dinner, he would push himself away from the table and promptly fall asleep on Jo's couch. Eventually, he felt comfortable enough to begin to share more of his life history.

This man – slowly transforming from one of stone to one of flesh and bone – would tell Jo of his time in the Russian Army. He ashamedly admitted that he had been ordered to shoot men, women, and children in the countries that Russia occupied. Lamenting over the futility of his life, he would confess that he just couldn't live with himself any longer. He described his dreams – nightmares, really – a reliving of his time in Russia.

Jo often talked to Mikhail about God. She told him of how He had sent his son Jesus to die for our sins. She would convey the truth, that Jesus could meet him right where he was. He did not need to clean his life up or make amends before he came to the Cross. He could lay his sins there, freed from their burden forever, and learn to live a life wholly and acceptable to God. It seemed as if Mikhail wanted to believe her, but something – some deeply held doubt – kept him from trusting in the message completely.

Mikhail continued to use his musical skills in church, to the glory of the One he had not yet come to know. He would play the piano, and my sister would play the organ. He would always leave after the singing, before the preaching would begin.

In time, he trusted Jo enough to allow her to see his condo. When he unlocked the door and swung it wide, she couldn't believe the mess she saw.

Mikhail's drinking did not allow him to think clearly, so his home – a reflection of his life – was in dire shape. Nothing was in its place. Dirty dishes – food cooked days and weeks before in pans and containers – lay all over the kitchen. Dirty laundry lay in piles here and there. The kitty litter desperately needed to be changed. Old newspapers and unopened mail overflowed every tabletop, and garbage overflowed every can. The bathrooms had not been cleaned, it seemed to Jo, in decades.

Jo convinced Mikhail to hire two cleaning ladies. It took them two weeks to organize and clean his condo.

Apparently, Mikhail's shopping habits were as erratic as his eating and living habits. The cleaning ladies found boxes and bags of items never used, new clothes never worn.

The newly organized condo could not deliver Mikhail from his disorganized mind. Late one night, as he sat home in another drunken stupor, two masked men broke in. They beat Mikhail severely. They stole his musical instruments, computers, and equipment. They took his cash, his jewelry, and anything else of value. When they left, he was in such bad shape that he had to crawl for help. His neighbors took one look at him and immediately called an ambulance and the police.

Mikhail spent a month in the hospital, unable to eat or move by himself. It took a month for him to dry out. When he was finally released from the hospital, he came to church and asked to be baptized and to make a profession of faith.

Jo called me, elated. When she told me the date of the

service, I promised to attend. We had been praying for Mikhail's conversion for so long. Could it be that our prayers had finally been answered?

Mikhail's Russian violinist friend came again, commanding her strings with bow and pluck as Mikhail hammered those buried within the wooden tomb of the piano. It was a beautiful service, the likes of which I might never hear again.

Mikhail looked like a changed man. He had trimmed his hair and beard and had taken to cleaning and pressing his clothes. I did not have to ask; his clear eyes and focused conversation told me that he had given up the bottle. His skin held a healthy glow, too. Mikhail had been transformed into a wonderful, sober Russian gentleman. He could not have done this on his own. He must truly have accepted the free gift of salvation and turned his life over to Christ.

In time, Mikhail fell in love with another Russian lady with a beautiful voice. The music they made together could make you laugh or cry.

I was anxious to learn more about this Russian man and his new, Christ-transformed life. Jo suggested that I invite him and his girlfriend up to Michigan to stay at my vacation cottage, and I readily agreed. On the appointed day, my family and I eagerly welcomed them. We had prepared a special dinner for them, and they rewarded us ten-fold with a performance of Russians songs afterwards – Mikhail sitting at a portable keyboard while his friend sang. Thankfully, I had thought to bring my video camera. The entire evening was mournfully beautiful, and the recording is among my most precious possessions.

The two left all too soon, and my entire family felt blessed by the experience. In appreciation for our hospitality, they surprised me by sending two dozen magnificent roses in various hues of purple, white, pink, yellow, and red.

I telephoned him to thank him for his beautiful gift. After

talking for a few minutes, Mikhail said that he had things he needed to discuss with me. He asked if I would go to dinner with him the next time I visited my sister. I had no idea what was on his mind, but I agreed to his invitation.

A few weeks later, I phoned Jo with the news of the visit I had planned. I asked her to let Mikhail know I was coming as well. Jo said that Mikhail had just left for Mexico for a short vacation but that she would tell him as soon as she saw him again.

The man never received my message.

One evening, a few days after Mikhail would have arrived in Mexico, Jo received some terrible news. She called me, distraught beyond comfort, and told me that Mikhail was dead. She said that he had apparently passed away after going down to the bar in the hotel and having a drink.

According to his girlfriend, Mikhail had been depressed in the days leading up to this event. They had gone to Mexico, hoping that the trip would lift his spirits. On the night of his death, Mikhail's girlfriend had grown tired and had fallen asleep. She said that she'd had no knowledge of his making a trip to the bar until she had learned of his death.

Mikhail had been a changed man before that trip. I knew he was. Yet, why was it that he could still not live with himself?

What really killed him? Would I have been able to help him if I could have gotten to him, talked to him, sooner?

I may never know the answers to these questions. Yet I cannot allow them to plague me. I must rest in the knowledge that I do have. Mikhail was transformed. I saw it happen. Watching him helped me see the love, the forgiveness, and the life-changing power of Jesus a little more clearly. That is enough.

The Seven Transformations of Peter DeHaan
By Peter DeHaan

A caterpillar turns into a butterfly; a tadpole becomes a frog. People can change, too. Here is my story.

One: We moved between fourth and fifth grade. I didn't learn much at my new school. I was far ahead in most subjects, especially Math. However, I lagged behind in English, especially grammar, sending me on a lifelong quest to grasp it. Given that I ended up a writer, and not a mathematician as planned, this ironic twist amuses me. How I managed to earn A's in English remains a mystery.

Teachers give more attention to students on the fringe, both those who struggle and those who shine. Since I stood out in most areas, my teacher gave me more attention. Although I didn't learn much academically that year, she gave me something more important, something life changing: an enhanced self-image.

Succinctly, I began fifth grade as an above-average student who believed he was average. I ended the year as an above-average student who believed he was exceptional. This single readjustment of my self-perception forever altered my life. No longer did I seek to merely get by in school, to take the easy way out. My attitude toward learning changed from drudgery to delight. I now desired to excel.

My newfound interest in education spilled over into religion, as I devoured faith-friendly books – both fiction and nonfiction. Later, I became intentional about reading the Bible. I loved my pursuit of biblical knowledge. Soon, I read the New Testament, and a couple of years later I devoured the entire Bible in one summer vacation. This sparked a life-long passion of digging for truth in God's word.

As strange as it sounds, a secular schoolteacher provided the catalyst for my first transformation: an overall desire to learn, which spilled over to an intellectual pursuit of God.

Two: I grew up attending two small, mainline denominational churches, where church was a traditional experience: stoic, reserved – and boring. I had trouble connecting faith with church. What I read in the Bible didn't much match what I experienced on Sunday. Perhaps changing churches would solve my dilemma.

After high school, I veered evangelical.

At this new church, aside from seeing young people my age excited about faith and happy to go to church, two other things astounded me: the music and the sermon. Both were fresh and inviting. This sparked a spiritual rejuvenation in me.

My old church had effectively put God in a box. As I migrated to a different doctrine, I had to escape my old theology. This resulted in a newfound freedom to comprehend God afresh. My faith leapt forward when I came to this church, completing a shift in my focus from an intellectual pursuit of God to a personal relationship with Jesus.

However, my new church also put God in a box, too: even smaller and more confining. Their box, fundamental in construction, lacked love and excelled at judgment. Their idea of godly living existed as rules. Theirs was a heavy load. Jesus proclaimed the opposite: a light burden and gentle yoke. He offered rest from the religious regulations of the day – not bondage to them.

This church's doctrine was dogmatic. They isolated themselves from most of Christianity, turning up their religious noses at the unity Jesus prayed for. At first, I didn't see their error, but when I did, it became an oppressive weight. A spiritual angst welled up inside; I craved escape. My second transformation occurred not when I joined this church or when I left it, but in the realization that Jesus' church is more than one gathering, one denomination, or even one faith perspective (be it mainline, evangelical, or charismatic – either Protestant or Catholic). The church of Jesus, with its many branches, is diverse and wonderful. He prayed we would be one – and I began to embrace that, too.

Jesus' church is huge – and I'm glad I'm part of it.

Three: I wasn't being fed spiritually, so I switched churches. My reason sounded so spiritual, but my claim revealed immaturity. Unable to feed myself, I expected my pastor to do it for me. I was a baby Christian, only able to drink milk and not eat solid food. Though I read the Bible daily, prayed most days, and had a relationship with Jesus, I expected my pastor to shovel enough spiritual sustenance into me each Sunday to sustain me for the week. I didn't know how to do this myself. Even worse, I didn't realize I was supposed to. After all, that's what we pay our ministers to do.

The pastor at this new church had a different view. He explained I needed to feed myself – and then showed me how. Soon I learned what to do, no longer relying on him to nourish me. I discovered how to listen to God, hearing his words and direction. I grew as a person of prayer and faith; my intimacy with God deepened, overwhelming me with peace and joy.

Learning to feed myself spiritually marked my third

transformation, establishing the basis for the next one.

Four: I met with a group of believers who diligently sought more from their faith. We immersed ourselves in learning about the Holy Spirit. I was ecstatic about the new truths we were learning. After a time, with my friends gathered around, I asked the Holy Spirit to indwell me, to take over my life, and envelop me. They stretched out their hands and prayed for me – and nothing happened.

What went wrong?

Discouraged over this non-event, only later did I realize I'd already done this.

Decades prior, while still in high school, one of the things I read was a little blue booklet called *The Four Spiritual Laws*. I studied it carefully and eagerly said the prayer they suggested. A few years later came a follow-up booklet that taught about living the spirit-filled life. I raced through it to reach the end, seeking what I needed to do. With excitement, I invited the Holy Spirit into my life and to fill me. A powerful wave of God's love engulfed me, a warm supernatural whoosh. Life made sense; everything came into focus. God emerged for me as a vibrant, real presence.

However, after a few days, my supernatural bliss evaporated; my spirit-filled euphoria was gone. Dejected, I returned to my tiny book to reclaim that feeling but without success. Eventually, I tossed it aside in disgust and soon forgot it.

Though I failed to comprehend it then, I later realized the Holy Spirit had been quietly active in my life ever since but without my awareness. I thought supernatural insights and promptings were normal for all Christians. Now that I understood the scope of His influence, I became intentional about listening and following the Holy Spirit's lead. Nowadays we work together as a team – at least, most of the time.

My fourth transformation embraced the person of the oft-forgotten member of the Trinity: the Holy Spirit.

Praise Father, Son, and Holy Spirit.

Five: The opportunity for another change came when a group of likeminded Jesus followers launched a healing room. This required a bold step forward, both for our group and for us individually. We went to training, and we practiced what we learned, initially on each other and eventually applying it to others, timidly at first and then with greater confidence – not in ourselves but in God's awesome power. Our faith in action moved forward. This stretched me spiritually, and I savored my new insights into God and the grandeur of who He is.

Jesus, we learned, came to heal *and* to save. Two thousand years ago, the masses clamored for his healing power, but they largely missed his saving power. Today, Christians in the Western world see Jesus as savior but largely dismiss him as healer. I embrace both – and with unapologetic passion.

Each week our team would gather to worship God and listen for His instructions. Then we'd open our doors to offer prayer and healing. There I experienced firsthand what I'd only read about. God used us to heal people: emotionally, spiritually, and physically – sometimes gradually and sometimes immediately.

As we worked together, we taught and encouraged one another, learning to rely on the Holy Spirit for direction and power. My fifth transformation had begun, never complete but always moving forward.

Six: I started college when I was sixteen. Twenty-seven years later, I finally finished – or so I thought – with a PhD in Business Administration. I never went full-time but always fit my classes and homework around a full-time job, usually while working forty-five to fifty-five hours a week.

Along the way, I made many sacrifices. To my dismay, this

included giving up time with family. When my diploma for my doctorate arrived, my wife asked, "Are you finally finished?" I assured her I was.

But God had other plans. A few years later, he whispered to me, "Go back to school." He didn't say when, where, or why. He simply said, "Go." I guess the rest was up to me. Since God was doing the telling, I figured my studies should have a spiritual focus. Both dismayed and elated at the prospect of more formal education, I moved forward, but my quest was a long one. It took five years, but I graduated with a second PhD, this one in Pastoral Ministry, of all things. My dissertation explored church unity. The topic drew me in with increasing fervor; I could not let go of its persistent grasp. The unity of Jesus' church became my passion.

Writing my dissertation also sparked something else deep inside my soul. Although I'd been writing most of my life, for the first time my writing intersected with my faith. Until then, I'd spent decades writing about business and for business. But now being a wordsmith had a greater purpose. I ceased trying to write quickly for work and began striving to write with quality for God. My words now had a higher calling.

My fervor to write about godly things exploded into a calling I could not shake. Soon I wondered if my next career would be as a writer. As I studied and practiced and improved, I knew verbalizing my intention was the next step.

At a mere whisper uttered in the privacy of my writing room, the words, "I am a writer" released an inner desire to write for God. Then I spoke, again, this time a little louder, "I am a writer." Self-doubt retreated. But I needed to make a firm declaration. "I am a writer!" I declared it with confidence. And so I was. My sixth transformation – as a writer on a mission for God – was set in motion.

Seven: I don't know what the future holds or the additional transformations awaiting me. There is one, however, I can be sure of: death.

I will one day die, and my ultimate transformation will take place. My body – where my soul and spirit reside – will cease to function. My essence will find release, no longer imprisoned in the physical realm, perhaps no longer bound by time. My spirit, the essential me, will transform into something wonderful, amazing, and everlasting – not for personal glory or self-aggrandizement but for eternal communion with my Creator, worshiping and experiencing true spiritual intimacy with the King of Transformation.

Then my transformations will be complete; I will finally be home.

Jesus-follower and wordsmith **Peter DeHaan** shares his passion for life and faith through words. Go to www.peterdehaan.com to read his blog "Spiritually Speaking," download his e-book *My Faith Manifesto*, receive his monthly newsletter, or connect via social media. Peter DeHaan has a PhD degree from Trinity College of the Bible and Trinity Theological Seminary, awarded "with high distinction." He is a top-twenty winner for *Imagine This! An ArtPrize Anthology*, published September 2013. Peter is an avid reader and podcast consumer. A movie buff who enjoys nature walks – though not at the same time – Peter celebrates both as sensory experiences that feed his inner muse. In his idle moments, he dreams of the day when pizza and popcorn are reclassified as major food groups. Peter and his wife live in Southwest Michigan. They have two married children, two grand puppies, and recently met their first grandchild.

Thank you for reading *The Transformation Project*. We hope you enjoyed and were encouraged by these stories of transformation. God continues to work in our lives as we focus on Him. Please, if possible, leave a review on what you have just read.

WWW.CONCERNINGLIFE.ORG

Our mission, at Concerning Life Publishing, LLC, is to deliver to the public, books that make a difference in the lives of the reader. We are a Christian publisher and our books have that flavor. We do not shy away from publishing Christian ideals and believe that there is a market for such books. We do believe that Jesus Christ changes lives through the written word.

Made in the USA
Charleston, SC
10 December 2013